GUIDANCE MONOGRAPH SERIES

SHELLEY C. STONE

BRUCE SHERTZER

Editors

GUIDANCE MONOGRAPH SERIES

The general purpose of Houghton Mifflin's Guidance Monograph Series is to provide high quality coverage of topics which are of abiding importance in contemporary counseling and guidance practice. In a rapidly expanding field of endeavor, change and innovation are inevitably present. A trend accompanying such growth is greater and greater specialization. Specialization results in an increased demand for materials which reflect current modifications in guidance practice while simultaneously treating the field in greater depth and detail than commonly found in textbooks and brief journal articles.

The list of eminent contributors to this series assures the reader expert treatment of the areas covered. The monographs are designed for consumers with varying familiarity to the counseling and guidance field. The editors believe that the series will be useful to experienced practitioners as well as beginning students. While these groups may use the monographs with somewhat different goals in mind, both will benefit from the treatment given to content areas.

The content areas treated have been selected because of specific criteria. Among them are timeliness, practicality, and persistency of the issues involved. Above all, the editors have attempted to select topics which are of major substantive concern to counseling and guidance personnel.

Shelley C. Stone

Bruce Shertzer

FAMILY
CONSULTATION

DANIEL W. FULLMER
UNIVERSITY OF HAWAII

HAROLD W. BERNARD
OREGON STATE SYSTEM OF HIGHER EDUCATION

HOUGHTON MIFFLIN COMPANY · BOSTON
NEW YORK · ATLANTA · GENEVA, ILL. · DALLAS · PALO ALTO

PREFACE

The individual receives his life sentence from the family. The school is designed by society to punctuate the sentence. The church or religious agency is designed to supply the capital letters, the underlining, and the italics. The community, including the neighborhood and the mass media, supply the adjectives to qualify the meanings within the sentence. It has been said that a wise man declares his sentence. Others live life as a question.

D. W. F.
H. W. B.

CONTENTS

EDITORS' INTRODUCTION

It has long been known that an individual's attitudes and behavior are markedly influenced by the family into which he was born and in which he develops to adulthood. The pattern established may be modified and changed, but probably never completely eradicated. Many behavioral deviations can be and often are traced to the subtleties of family relationships.

Family consultation has but recently begun to receive attention in counselor education programs. The area is of import because of its yield in knowledge and counselor practices. Many textbooks in the counseling field have emphasized the individual's development in relation to school. This has tended to place too much stress upon a single factor in his environment with little recognition given to the obvious fact that *both* family and school affect the socialization of children. This monograph seeks to correct the notion that the child learns only at school or only at home. Rather, the assumption is that he learns from both. The family as a learning model is viewed and examined by the two authors.

Daniel Fullmer and Harold Bernard introduced family consultation into counselor education through the NDEA Counseling and Guidance Institute preparation programs conducted at the Oregon State System of Higher Education (Portland, Oregon). Undoubtedly they have had more experience in teaching, demonstrating, supervising, and conducting family consultation within the context of school counselor preparation than any other individuals within the United States. In short, their knowledge and experience in this area provide an unmatched resource for authorship of this monograph.

In our judgment, counseling practitioners and counselors in preparation will find that *Family Consultation* contains not only much that will interest them but more that will aid them of an immediate and enduring nature.

SHELLEY C. STONE

BRUCE SHERTZER

AUTHORS' INTRODUCTION

Which person has been designated as the one who needs help? Which individual is excluded emotionally from the others in the family? Is there alienation between the parents? Is any individual alienated from any other individual or from the family group as a whole? Is the child used as a communication link between parents? Is the child used to fill an emotional void? Is the child used as a narcissistic extension of the parent(s)?

The family pattern for "touching" each other, both physically and psychologically, may be the most revealing source of meaningful observations available to counselors. Human beings engage in a wide range of contact or touching behavior. Adult human activities may range from physical stroking of a loved one to symbolic abstract "touching" characterized by verbal recognition. The counselor can learn to read such seemingly non-contextual cues. The non-verbal and non-contextual behavior is included as relevant material when making interpretations of verbalized communication in family consultation. The all-at-once character of behavior in face-to-face family consultation may be quite a contrast to sequential written descriptions of counseling session behavior. One may tolerate the shock if one is prepared adequately for it.

D. W. F.
H. W. B.

Introduction

Family consultation is a form of family education using conditions similar to classroom teaching and learning. The chief difference between it and family psychotherapy lies in the focus or emphasis in the process of treatment. Family consultation focuses upon a patient, or one member of a family identified by some means, as the reason for being in treatment. The "all-at-once" nature of family consultation is a considerable contrast with the sequential nature of conventional group or individual counseling procedures. The emphasis in the monograph is upon the *method* of family consultation.

The assumptions made are consistent with the culture. Family consultation proceeds only with the permission of the family. A family actively in a crisis seeks help and becomes engaged in consultation more often than families between crises. It is assumed that all families experience crises during which they may need help. We assume the school to be a source of help. The school is best prepared to engage a family in educational activities. First-aid for family crises is not the school's primary function although many personal emergencies are handled by teachers and counselors daily. Family consultation will not eliminate crises, but family members may learn to handle the exigencies of a crisis more proficiently. The goal of family consultation is to help a family gain the fuller realization of its potential for learning. The healthy family is the most productive learning model in the culture. This is the key assumption behind family consultation.

The method of family consultation assumes that the family is a learning model for socialization and cultural inculcation. The assumptions include references to what a family *is* and to what a family *does*. Extensive, in-depth discussion of these assumptions would require much more space than is available. Family consultation is unique because it deals with normal families having normal difficulties. The chief function is one of prevention. Secondarily, family consultation may be corrective and remedial.

Interaction Distortions

Distortion in family interaction is found in the communication patterns of families in trouble. Families in trouble rarely show their disturbances to the outside world. Usually the only symptoms that surface are acting-out behaviors of the family member(s) in trouble. Often families resist joining consultation groups because they fear that their interaction distortions will be revealed. Distortion of interaction is necessary if one or more members of a family are acting-out. The school counselor often is confronted with maladaptive behavior from youngsters who are generalizing family interaction distortions to the larger society. Such youngsters rarely understand the nature of the negative reaction they get from other persons. They only know that the concepts they have are closely tied to their identity and personal meanings. Motivations are intense under such conditions because changing behavior or ceasing controversial acts is too threatening to the individual's personal meaning. Within a family, each individual demands that someone fill "my" needs. Demands must be met, since this is a basic purpose of the family. Rules and rituals are developed by a family to serve the needs of each member. The demands of privileged persons get met first. Privileged status is sought and maintained by alignments, loyalties, peer groups, mutuality pacts, power distributions, and deviant behavior.

Within the struggle to maintain its integrity, a family and its individual members tend to follow certain basic common learning patterns. Following patterns is an attempt to systematize some of the kinds of concerns and conditions that affect a family and its interaction patterns. By listening to the interaction pattern of a family, following its distortions, myths, fantasies, hopes and aspirations, and basic realities, counselors can begin to see the meanings each individual derives from the family. (Schofield, 1966)

Alignment Within a Family

Whose side are you on? This question is heard over and over again within the interaction pattern of a family. The basic alignment in every family has to start with a man and a woman who marry. In our culture, if there is no marriage, the family is basically an illegitimate group. Alignment must begin on a tentative contract basis. Maintaining the alignment between the man and the woman over a period of time requires a complicated pattern of interactions. Each makes certain demands upon the other to fill his or her needs within the structure. The addition of individual members (children) obviously complicates the alignment.

Alignments change as situations alter. For instance, in certain situations, the mother and the father may be in alignment; in certain "other" situations, the siblings may be in alignment; or there may be combinations of a parent and certain siblings in alignment, against or with certain "other" conditions or persons within the family group. These alignments are always known to the participants and therefore must be made clear to the counselors through direct questioning. The counselors need to know the situations and the alignments as members take sides.

Loyalties Within a Family

The loyalties maintained within the family group are extremely significant if counselors are to help members learn new ways of meeting their problem conditions. The primary loyalty in a family is to the family as a group, not to any individual within or among the family. The healthy family seems to have a very consistent and strong loyalty tie binding each individual member to the family group. A family that trades in individual personal loyalties may discover that persons *outside* the family have higher saliency than do persons *within* the family. Such conditions create conflicts that become central to the inability of a family to meet its continuing needs. The healthy family provides youngsters with an ability to leave intra-family loyalties behind as they mature. Each goes forth and reproduces a similar model — a healthy family. Counselors should discover as early as possible the extent, nature, and types of loyalties that are expressed within and among family members and external significant others.

Peer Groups Within A Family

Peer groups are important because they form the basic socialization units within our society. Reference groups and peer groups become the central source of values, valuing, validation, and viability within our society.

Parent peer groups are important because without them parents have no basic adult source of values against which to compare their behavior. Parents need their own reference groups in order to maintain a continuing evaluation of their behavior, their standards, and their attitudes and values. Youngsters within a family form what are called *sibling peer groups*. There may also be individuals who have no peer group within the family. The person who is designated as the family problem usually is without peer group status among his siblings. The counselor should very quickly differentiate the kinds of peer groups that exist among the siblings and the kinds of peer groups to which children belong outside of the family structure. External peer groups are important because they provide the source of confirmation of values and standards relatively independent of the family.

Pseudo-mutuality

A family consists of people who have decided to live together in a mutually cooperative venture. If being mutual means that each individual must be able to share something important, it leads to a kind of constant and strong contract for real mutuality. If anything interferes with this process, if either individual partner within a marriage somehow "fakes it," the other person often is left emotionally suspended. *Pseudo-mutuality* is seen as a kind of pretense at a role instead of a real-live-being-myself role. An example of pseudo-mutuality is found in men who maintain a mistress or women who keep an auxiliary lover.

Emotional Divorce

One of the most difficult conditions with which we have attempted to deal in family consultation results when two people stay together even though, emotionally, they are divorced. The family maintained under these conditions creates numerous crises for its youngsters. An individual *identity crisis* is only one of the kinds of difficulties youngsters face. If parents cohabitate in a state of emotional divorce, there are additional social impacts each youngster confronts as he matures. It is only with great difficulty that such problems can be reconciled with the basic standards of our culture when a pretense of the marriage is maintained by parents.

A mother will say, "But, we must stay together to maintain a home for the children." Statements of this sort place counselors in a position of conflict with the culture. Because counselors do represent the cultural values, accepting behavior in the face of a condition called emotional divorce is akin to self-incrimination.

Narcissistic Pact

A narcissistic pact is about the most insidious kind of primitive contract two people can arrange. Supposedly, a family is a group in which individuals can grow and prosper. If the parent relationship is merely a narcissistic pact, there is no "dividend production" that can be used by the youngsters. In such a family, the parents must use all of their energies and efforts to meet the needs of each other so that a continuing relationship can be maintained. Jealousy within the family is the key in discovering the existence of a narcissistic pact. Counselors will recognize the inappropriateness with which each member of the pact reacts to efforts by others to form a relationship with another person.

Power Distribution Between Parents

If the parental relationship involves a power struggle, the use of the power by one or both parents can have a profound effect upon the developments of the youngsters in the home. Counselors should determine very early the level of power that can be exercised by each parent. A common expression heard in family consultation is: "I'm the one to blame for this condition. It is all my fault." The usual counselor response used in the face of this statement, "No, if you had that much power, you would have handled it differently and you would not need to be here. What we see is that you do not have enough power to do anything different from what you are doing."

The level of power may approach zero. Counselors should look carefully at the positiveness or the negativeness of the power exerted by one parent or another. Notice the regard each partner has for the other. The reasons for maintaining the relationship are sometimes expressed in the quality of the regard.

Counselors use the culturally accepted role expectations for fathers and mothers to estimate both the amount of power and its distribution between the parents. Often, it is the reluctance to use any power because of its attendant responsibility and accountability that leads parents to get into difficulty with their youngsters. The parent may be afraid to block the youngster's acting-out behavior because he fears his own ignorance regarding the way his actions will affect the youngster. One of the common misuses of power which is a great concern to parents is in the use of power to punish instead of using power *to set limits*. Our position has been to encourage parents to use their power to set limits and to avoid using power to punish youngsters.

A parent exhibits punishing behavior when he acts out his own emotions and exacts a price from himself for correcting the youngster. In setting a limit, the parent remains in control of his own emotions and merely becomes adamant concerning a certain expectation that has been placed in the youngster's path.

Affective Mass

A youngster is born into a family in which he must gain enough identity to permit him to find his own self away from the family. He must thread his way through family myths and delusions, the use of illogical modes of thinking, the inappropriate and appropriate distribution of affect to discover the structure and meaning in adult life. Often, a youngster must free himself from symbiotic attachments in order to attain his identity. A symbiotic attachment is a kind of interpersonal relationship where one person, usually the mother, will feed upon the narcissistic extension of herself, usually a son. The boy is taught to meet the emotional needs of the mother by the demands of very close person-to-person ties. Symbiotic attachment may also exist between a parent and a grandparent. Schofield (1966) has called this "malignant mothering" which is merely an extension into adult life of a symbiotic relationship existing in childhood. This is one of many examples of a kind of continuity between early childhood behavior and learning.

If, within a family structure, the affective mass is focused upon one individual so that all demands for certain kinds of need fulfillment are made upon one person, that individual may become disturbed or be extremely disadvantaged and handicapped within the family structure. A presenting problem usually includes this kind of circumstance. Whether or not the youngster is a scapegoat for an adequate personal development on the part of a parent or parents is a question that must be answered in the minds of the counselors early in the counseling relationship. Without this information, the counselor proceeds without any accurate knowledge about relationships between individuals within the family.

2

Diverse Ways for
Meeting Common Needs

The family is man's oldest, most pervasive, and most persistent institution. As the most powerful factor in the development of the human personality — for learning how to be human rather than animal — it has received and still receives much attention. At times, this attention is laudatory, at times censorious, or merely descriptive. In primitive societies, the attention was in the form of folklore, tradition, ceremony, and ritual. In contemporary society, the family is studied by anthropologists, sociologists, and psychologists. Also, it is of great interest to economists, educators, churchmen, social workers, criminologists, and those in the health professions. The family is, of course, of deep and intimate concern to all those who live, have lived, or would like to live within its confines.

A family brings together, in intimate association, persons varying widely in age, having different abilities, performing a wide variety of functions, and pursuing distinctly different goals. Yet, it is expected that these differences will be so clearly perceived and so sincerely and mutually accepted by its members that harmony in interrelationships will prevail. However, this is not necessarily or even frequently the case. A difference between the healthy and the disturbed family is that the former has achieved some technique for resolving the problems incident to intimate association, while, in the other, the problems remain chronic or continue to build in the absence of adequate coping behavior. The difficulty, from a sociological or psychological point of view, is not with the family as an institution, but with the manner in which it functions. It can be said, as it has been said of other problems, "The trouble with the family is us."

One purpose of this chapter is to describe the approaches to the study of family which are made by anthropologists, sociologists, and psychologists. In this context, it is not, however, the method of study that is important, but the conclusions that have been derived from the studies. Unfortunately, from a purely academic viewpoint, it is not as easy to distinguish a particular bit of knowledge as being anthropological, sociological, or psychological, as it is to describe the purpose and methods as belonging to one discipline or another.

The study of the family by various disciplines is, of course, important in that it allows us to examine more closely all the facets of family functioning so the counselor can understand the multitude of forces with which he works. He should know what dynamics are involved; what beliefs, sanctions, and roles are involved; and what the potentialities and pitfalls of intervening in family processes are.

The study of the family is based on the assumptions that our "human nature" is learned; that the major environment for learning to be "human" is the family; and that, because family living is a learned response, there may be better ways to live within a family. Anthropologists have shown that there are different ways to live within a family. These ways are not necessarily superior or inferior except in the context of a culture. Similarly, the counselor's purpose is to implant the idea during consultation that there are different ways to behave in a family, some of which are superior to others. Unfortunately, in our society, there are instances in which certain individuals are deprived of access to adequate learning experiences relative to family living. These persons may be handicapped by what they do not know (e.g., see reference below to the Negro family) and the challenge is presented for providing a productive model for learning. An approach to meeting this challenge is present in family counseling and in family group consultation.

After reviewing some of the aspects of life which show how culture influences behavior, and stressing the fact that there is much individual variation in behavior, L. K. Frank (1948) made a cogent statement regarding personality formation:

> From the very beginning of life the newborn infant is called upon to
> adjust his "internal environment" to the demands and requirements of

the culture into which he has been born. After having been continuously nourished in utero, he has to adjust himself at birth to whatever practice of feeding is customary in the culture into which he has been born. In some cultures he is kept at the breast almost continuously; in others, he has to accomodate himself to a four-hour feeding schedule. He is required to transform his biological hunger into a patterned appetite which will enable him to find sustenance and enjoyment in the kind of food which his parents think desirable, eaten at the intervals they prescribe.

When a child is fed whenever he is hungry, he gets more than food — he gets a feeling of confidence that his needs are going to be met; he feels that he can trust this world. As all the successive difficult lessons of social adjustment come along, he has this basic security and confidence to build upon. If, on the other hand, he is left hungry and thwarted by an inflexible feeding schedule, he may begin to doubt and fear the world, and is likely to approach his subsequent experiences with doubt, fear, and insecurity.

The Anthropological Approach

Anthropology has suddenly become fashionable as its practitioners have returned from the study of other societies to report on the inconsistencies and variations in the ways man thinks, values, and lives. Its practitioners have shown the consistencies and variations which exist between the past and present. The knowledge derived is of both practical and of academic interest. Kluckhohn (1959) asserts that there are four unifying factors in the anthropological approach: (1) focus on man's variations and similarities, (2) adherence to a comparative point of view, (3) a conviction that there is a relationship between man's history, physique, way of life, and language, that is discernible, and (4) an assumption that man's rational life can only be understood when concomitantly studied with his nonrational and irrational behavior.

The universality of the family may be documented from many studies and such documentation is illustrated in the material by Mead and Heyman (1965). The family, in some form, is found in every known successful culture or society which man has created. No enduring and successful substitute for the family has yet been found, though the experimentation still continues. Currently experimentation includes the state-controlled techniques for raising children which is called the *kibbutz* in Israel and the *commune* in the People's Republic of China. Mead and Heyman observe that such state-controlled substitutes wither and return to the conventional family, or perish, as was the case with the Incas of Peru.

The anthropologist's evaluation of the family might be paralleled by the Harlows' (1962) experiments on monkeys in psychology. The Harlows found that raising young monkeys in the prolonged absence of the mother resulted in the development of sexually and socially inadequate monkeys. We also know that some human mothers are inadequate and that some foster mothers are excellent influences on child development. Hence, it would seem that the *kibbutz* and *commune* have the ingredients for success as long as the proportion of adults to children and male-female ratio of parental substitutes remains adequate. Some of the economic and educational aspects of the family may still be questioned, but apparently the reproductive function is not hampered by lack of the formalized family.

Spiro (1960) argued that the *kibbutz* is actually a stronger institution than is marriage and that it is, in effect, an extended family. Because it includes a common domicile for both sexes, it entails interaction between the sexes, it involves emotional intimacy, it establishes — at least ideally — an exclusive sexual relationship, and leads to the deliberate choice to have children. Spiro regards the *kibbutz* as a unique kind of family. And, with this orientation, he agrees with Mead and others that the family is still universal.

The conclusions regarding the universality of the family are summarized by Murdock (1960) — although there is enough variation throughout the world that other investigators using different samplings might emphasize different elements in their conclusions. Murdock indicates that the nuclear family (consisting of man and wife and, typically, their offspring) is universal, but may be expanded by customs of polygamy (two or more nuclear families affiliated by plural marriage) or the extended family (extended by parent-child-relatives relationships).

On the basis of the study of 250 human societies, Murdock indicates four functions fundamental to human social life that are served by the nuclear family. These are the sexual, economic, reproductive, and educational aspects of life. Sex and reproduction are essential to life itself, and without education culture would be terminated. Looking at the variations within the continuity of the nuclear family, it may be noted that different societies define sexual taboos and permissions in a variety of manners — the universal aspect being that husband and wife are not denied sexual access to one another. One society, the Banaro of New Guinea, comes closest to being an exception to this by forbidding the groom to approach his young wife until she bears a child by a special sib-friend of his father. In none of these societies is sexual activity without restraint, but, also, without exception, some measure of sexual liberty, says Murdock, is granted to husband and wife (e.g., the tacit sanction implied by the double standard) of the nuclear family. Marriage, by virtue of its surrounding the powerful drive of sex with many taboos and privileges, reinforces the many responses which precede and follow sexual intercourse. Thus, many of man's actions and habits are strengthened by marriage and family customs; and the family becomes such an integral part of living that its disturbance entails a major threat to a satisfying and productive life.

The economic aspects of the family appear to stem from the biology of male and female. Men, being physically stronger, have tended to do the heavier work — lumbering, mining, land clearance, housebuilding. Women, being restricted by menstruation, pregnancy, child-bearing, and child-rearing, have tended to do the lighter work — mending, cooking, gathering crops. However, it should be noted that the lines of distinction are broad rather than sharp. Custom, need, beliefs, and concepts result in many variations regarding the male as contrasted to the female economic role. For example, one may note the entry of women into the so-called man's role in American culture — law, medicine, and, more recently, engineering. One change which undoubtedly has much impact on the American family is the increasing number of women in the labor force. In 1920, women constituted 20 percent of the working population. In 1960, this number had risen to 32 percent and by 1970, it is estimated, will be 34 percent (*American Women,* 1963).

The rearing of children is, like the nature of the union of man and wife, known to have much variation. In some societies, men take a much more active part in child-rearing than in our own culture; in others, their role is even less. In some societies, older children assume much more responsibility for the younger child's care than we could grant in our own society. Psychologists, along with anthropologists, have made studies of the contrasting methods of weaning, toilet training, and disciplinary practices in an attempt to pinpoint the crucial forces in personality development. The major conclusions regarding these differences are that these practices stem in part from local geographic factors and economic needs. It is also concluded that what is done is less important than how and by whom it is done. This latter conclusion has potential significance for the counselor. For example, many persons have been alarmed about the influence of broken homes on children. Others take the view that disrupted, intact homes may have a more traumatic effect than do those that are actually broken. The implication of this view is that a widow or a divorcee may be a very fine parent even without the presence of a mate. It is conceivable that a mother may be a negative influence on children as long as her husband is around to keep her tense, angry, or frightened; then, upon the demise or departure of the husband, she may be able to control her behavior (or simply be herself) and become a salutary influence on the children. It is probable that, just as frequently, it is the woman whose absence will be a blessing for the father and the children. This may be the result of knowing that *now* one has to take responsibility, or it may be a matter of just getting rid of a constant source of emotional disruption. In short, the myth of motherhood must be viewed objectively. In some societies, the children of a particular father or mother are raised by the brother and his wife. Or, child-rearing may be performed by the parents of the real mothers and fathers — or at least by a different generation of adults.

Thus, anthropological studies suggest that some of the things that happen to families, and particularly to children, are not necessarily so foreboding as the pessimist is likely to suggest. There is considerable concern expressed regarding the effect of working mothers. There are those who wish for a return to the "good old days," when the father spent more time with his boys, teaching them the trade which would make them contributing citizens. As the son learned to be a farmer, saddle-maker, chandler, merchant, shipwright, he was also learning — by example — how to be a male. Today the father leaves the home early in the morning and returns late in the day (unless he is taking a road trip for a week or so). He is then too tired to spend much time with the children who quietly learn that father must not be disturbed. The consequence is that the male influence is pretty well omitted from the lives of growing children — a fact which is regarded as detrimental to both boys and girls. Regardless of the basic causes of broken homes — the absence of the male figure in the home or a woman's working — the fact remains for the counselor that these represent existing conditions. The authors of this monograph view these phenomena as being significant new challenges to learning.

Besides women's entry into the labor force and the physical removal of the father from the home, Coleman (1965) mentions some other changes which are of interest when interpreted in the light of anthropological data. One of these changes is the fact of geographical mobility. Families today move several times — from a small apartment as newly-weds to a suburban home as children are born, to a suburban area of larger homes as the family prospers, and finally, as retired persons, back to an apartment. This family movement results in a difficulty which may be met somewhat better by children than by adults — namely, loss of close friendships. The children do form new peer friendships, but contact between adults is more difficult and tenuous.

An outstanding example of variation in family pattern exists within American culture in the matriarchal family of the lower class Negro.

This, according to Frazier (1939), is recognized by relatively few persons. The middle-class Negro family is much like the family of the middle-class white family; but the lower-class Negro family typically lacks an adult male figure of significance. That this stems from the days of slavery, when families were split apart on the auction block with no concern on the part of whites, does not alter the fact that, at some time, the majority of Negro children (of all classes) have lived without a father or father substitute. In 1964, in about 25 percent of Negro families, the husband was absent by virtue of desertion, separation, or divorce (U.S. Bureau of Census, 1964), with some variation among geographical regions. Moreover, this figure is unchanged since 1950. At the same time, about 29 percent of Negro males were unemployed or not steadily employed. Thus, there is great probability that, at some time, the majority of Negro children have lived without the presence of an adequate male model.

It is recognized, at least in American culture, that productive work is a factor conducive to self-confidence, personality stability, and personal, as well as social, satisfaction. Work is the binding factor back of the successful person and is a requisite for those who carry on the dominant culture. A now anonymous person has said, "In the working life alone is to be found lasting satisfaction for the soul and the hope of salvation for mankind." Again, in the lower-class Negro family, where men and women are denied the opportunity for full participation in the work world, one sees the roots of alienation. To the extent that personal inadequacy and curtailed education are causes of nonparticipation, those things that can be done to stimulate personal adequacy are to be valued. Breaking the cycle of felt inadequacy is part of the task of family consultation.

In such data as the above we see the sources of the perpetuation of self-defeating behavior. The need for breaking the circular pattern of personal inadequacy is obvious. We see the exemplification of the fact that personality patterns are largely formed in the early years (*The Negro Family*, 1965). More specifically, the outcome, when combined with other factors, such as discrimination, poverty, unemployment, is a set of dismaying and discouraging statistics. Illegitimacy (over 25 percent of all Negro births in some cities), economic dependency, high and increasing rates of delinquency and crime, and high incidence of drug addiction are symptoms of dangerous social inadequacy (Pettigrew, 1964).

If one concedes the significance of the family and admits that the school is the institution which is most likely to reach all children, then the potential impact of family consultation as a school function might well be considered. The problem of inadequacy will not be entirely resolved, but the lives of many might well be influenced for the better.

Changes in patterns of living, as shown above, and the extremes perceived in the Negro family suggest some of the issues which are encountered in family consultation. Patterns of dating, particularly going steady, the growing importance of the school as a focal point in the child's life, the increasing significance of peer influences, the absence or insignificance of the father are all topics which make communication between parents and children difficult. The rate at which sophistication is achieved, says Coleman (1965), is a major problem for schools and, it would seem, for the parents who become anxious about the welfare of their offspring.

The Sociological Approach

It is difficult to distinguish between the anthropologist's contribution to the understanding of people and that made by sociologists. Dictionary definitions fail to make a clear differentiation in that anthropology is defined as the science of man, and sociology is defined as the study of human groups or social organizations. Kelly (1959) asserts that anthropology has come to designate the study of man in primitive societies. This study involves the three approaches of physical anthropology, linguistics, and cultural anthropology. The latter, concentrating on social organizations, value systems, art, and technology, is very much like sociology because sociology is defined as the study of the structure, function, dynamics, and relations of human groups to value systems, art, and technology. The matter is somewhat akin to the defining of intelligence, one definition of which is "intelligence is what intelligence tests measure." The statement has considerable serious merit and it seems that sociology (or anthropology) is what sociologists (or anthropologists) study.

Because of the growing realization of the complexity of behavior, the interrelatedness of various sciences, and the essential continuity and contiguity of man's life, the integration of the behavioral sciences is vigorously sought. Simple answers to man's behavior cannot realistically be sought, and the contributions of a single science will not suffice. The insights and emphases made by particular sciences are valuable, but the data provided must be correlated with complementary and supplementary data. Bronfenbrenner (1963) predicts not only that correlation of the behavioral sciences will be a goal, but that there will be a continuation of an already active transition toward closer correlation of intrinsic growth factors and situational factors; i.e., the life sciences will be correlated with the social sciences.

The need for integration of the various behavioral sciences is recognized in the establishment of new departments and coordination between traditional departments in universities. Graduate programs now emphasize such things as biochemistry and social psychology. The Center for Advanced Study in the Behavioral Sciences, begun in 1952 with support from the Ford Foundation, is an example. It annually subsidizes the postdoctoral study of fifty scholars from various fields and colleges and emphasizes the integration of various disciplines (Tyler, 1956).

Sociologists, interested in the matter of correlating the sciences and in the interactions which are taking place within a society, have, of course, focused some attention on the family. While the anthropologist is interested in comparative cultures, i.e., the variation *between* cultures, the sociologist places primary emphasis on the interactions *within* a culture. Actually, the distinctions are more academic than they are functional. For instance, both disciplines are concerned with the nature and functioning of the family, and both have noted the same changes in structure and in interaction.

One change, noted by sociologists, is the decreasing importance of the nuclear family in the United States. The nuclear family is a group composed of a man and a woman joined in a socially recognized partnership, together with their children (Bell and Vogel, 1960). In contrast to the nuclear family, there is the extended family, which consists of others in addition to the nuclear family — adult brothers and sisters, parents of the parents, cousins, etc. There has been a tendency to think of the nuclear and extended families as the models which characterize the modern American family. Fellin (1964) however, suggests that there are other family models which are significant. He refers to the modified extended family, which includes brothers, cousins, parents, etc., who do not live in the same house. In fact, they may not even live in the same city. The significant thing is that the members keep in close touch and are ready to give aid in the event of need. Litwak (1960) has also shown that the modified extended family can interrupt the tendency toward isolation which is set in motion by geographic mobility and the lack of nepotism in occupations. The alternative to receiving support from one's relatives is to depend on social institutions other than the family. The personnel of these other social institutions are social case workers, marriage counselors, the public school personnel, and, on a small and experimental scale, the family consultation counselors.

Many changes, usually the ones deplored by society, which have had a profound influence on children, were begun during World War II with what were known as "latchkey" children. With industry and business booming, there was an opportunity and a necessity for mothers to work to supplement the husband's military, or other, income. The war effort set a social expectation itself and work for women became the "thing to do." Children of school age were given a house key and had to assume responsibility for getting to and from school, for getting their own lunches, doing household chores, organizing their leisure, and sometimes getting themselves to bed on time. Cessation of World War II has not seemed significantly to interrupt this pattern, and the number of day-care child centers has steadily risen. However, the number is grossly inadequate. Across the nation, licensed day-care centers in 1960 were available to only 185,000 children, while there were three million mothers of children under six who were working outside the home (*American Women,* 1963).

With anthropologists charting the way to a realization of distinctly different, but provincially quite normal, ways of family behavior, it is instructive to see the implications of socioeconomic status for the family. Educators and sociologists have also, in the past few years, provided some valuable insights, but not without raising many questions. Riessman (1962) for example, indicates, as does Litwak (1960), that there is a temptation to overlook the positive forces that may exist to offset the mother's working outside the home. These same forces may tend to compensate for divorce, separation, desertion, or death of one of the parents. Thus, among the culturally deprived, a broken home need not imply family disorganization. With many children and hurried parents, the young have much time to spend together. There is much less concern about individualism and self concern than is the case in small families and with parents who give children more time.

The Psychological Approach

Historically, most of the professionals who have worked with families have been concerned with pathology. Traditionally, social work has been engaged in dealing with the economically inadequate. Psychologists have been concerned with the unhealthy family and quite often with the impact of such families on the individual. Educators have been concerned about families whose children are disturbing influences in the school, or children whose achievement is below their indicated level of ability. At least some of the foregoing concerns have shifted to an interest in the healthy family as a learning model, and family consultation is seen as a method of family education for those families experiencing only minor or normal difficulties, as well as for those which are having considerable difficulty.

The psychological approach to the family focuses upon the interpersonal reactions which take place within the home. The data used may be much the same as those used by the sociologist and the anthropologist, but the interpretations seem to vary to some extent. The emphasis is upon the emotional reaction and perception of the individuals concerned. One might regard the task of the psychologist as that of integrating and reconciling the data provided by sociology and anthropology, though contemporary studies by the latter two might well indicate that such integration is also within their province (Bernard, 1966).

There has been considerable interest in child-rearing practices — weaning, toilet training, discipline — as a function of socioeconomic status and also simply as a factor in personality formation. The results, both as to social class differences and as to the effects on the child's personality, are equivocal. Infants may be weaned as early as four months or as late as two or three years. Weaning may not be a function of age at all, but rather a matter of the child's maturation, he develops to the point that he can accommodate his hunger to the schedule of meals that is customary in a family or grows teeth that make nursing painful to the mother. Weaning may be a function of the mother's condition — drying up of her milk, another pregnancy, or simply a matter of her personal convenience. Despite intensive studies, no dependable conclusions have been reached. Because of paradoxical effects on personality, it seems that age at time of weaning is of no practical significance. There is a tendency today to think more of the mother's attitude and the total family milieu than of the child's age at the time of weaning or of the suddenness or gradualness of the weaning. If the mother's attitude is one of love and tenderness, the baby can abandon the bottle or the breast with no trauma. However, late weaning accompanied by disinterest or revulsion on the mother's part may be traumatic to the child. If siblings and father add to the feeling of acceptance, the infant can accommodate to sudden or early weaning with a minimum of discomfort. This is not to say that particular training practices have no effect on personality formation and social adjustment. It is simply recognizing that there are so many variables, particularly those pertaining to the overall home atmosphere, which are related to such things as weaning, discipline, and toilet training, that simple and single answers are not sound (Caldwell, 1964).

Among the factors that condition the relationship between mother and child is the quality of the relationship between husband and wife. Husband-wife felicity, at least in our culture, is so important that only an extremely stable mother (or father, if he is left with the maternal role) can be loving and accepting to children when anxiety, tension, anger, hostility, jealousy, and the like pervade the husband-wife relationship. It is the steady, consistent, chronic, characteristic atmosphere of the home that forms personality and prepares the infant, baby, and child for the series of developmental tasks that must be pursued throughout their lifetime (Bernard, 1966). Emotional "set" must be taken into account in all behavior and misbehavior. In the psychiatric clinic and family consultation sessions in the school setting, it has been repeatedly demonstrated that such mechanisms as projection, identification, and displacement, work to the disadvantage of children when parents are in chronic disagreement. This disagreement is frequently so pervasive and distressing that the defense of "staying together for the sake of the children" is of extremely dubious value. It is exactly at this point that family consultation, as a way of *looking at what is happening,* becomes significant to all participants — parents and children. Additionally, family group consultation is significant because members of one family can so readily see the mistakes made by another family — even though the mistakes are actually quite like their own (Hall, 1959).

One of the pervasive considerations, closely related to mother-child and husband-wife relations, which concerns the psychologist is that of the self-concept. Self-concept consists of the feeling that one has about how one can and will cope with the external forces one encounters in daily living. The self-concept was of concern in the New Testament of the Hindu Scriptures in the first century B.C. It is an important focus in the personality theory of Maslow (1954) and Combs and Snygg (1959). It is also basic in one of the major theories of the nature of an individual's career development (Super, 1963). There are without doubt, other orientations regarding personality formation in the family milieu, but the self-concept viewpoint is especially helpful.

Bell and Vogel (1960) report that much of the literature on the family focuses on mother-and-child relationships. Without denying the value of such an approach, they recognize the importance of giving attention to the family pattern as a whole. Four functional subsystems within the family merit consideration: (1) The *task activities* of the family — such things as providing food, shelter, gaining possessions, and the division of labor for exercising these functions — are a part of the personality formation influences. (2) The matter of *family leadership and coordination of authority* has wide-ranging impact on personality. This function is particularly noticeable when authority roles are equivocal or inappropriate, because the child's chance for the establishment of identity is confused. (3) *Family integration and solidarity* are basic to the process of socialization. Although stable personalities can tolerate a wide range of degrees of integration, either too much or too little family integration can have disorganizing effects. Strong families might be said to be those which are capable of finding alternate modes of maintaining solidarity. (4) The *family value system* provides the means by which the individual discovers direction and the source from which he internalizes his own value system. When the family value system is consistent and when there is consistent affirmation of those values, the individual develops dependable and rewarding behaviors. When the family values are inconsistent and behaviors are sporadically rewarded, there is an attendant inconsistency in which the individual perpetuates ineffectual and self-defeating behaviors.

Family consultation is designed and exercised to interrupt self-defeating, perpetuated patterns of family living. By getting family members to discuss and describe as accurately as possible what goes on in the family, new ways of self-perception may be achieved (Hall, 1959). When one family member describes how he feels, other family members may be helped to see how their behavior influences others; particularly they may see that the message they transmit by words is not the same as the message they transmit by action and a kind of double-bind may result. The presence of other persons helps those who are talking to phrase their words more logically and impersonally and less emotionally and personally. The presence of individuals from outside the family encourages family members to listen to what they themselves are saying. In family group consultation, one family in need of help can help another to achieve a different perspective. The evaluation given by other families in difficulty seems to be more acceptable than that given by a counselor who is viewed as not really knowing "how things are" in a family experiencing difficulty. Thus, each family perceives in another a model that provides some valuable orientation for change. Strange as it may seem, one family can perceive the errors made by another much more readily than it can see (or admit) its own inadequacies (Hall, 1959). Finally, an incentive and a means for contact with others is provided in family group consultation. It has been noted that families in trouble tend to become isolated from others. Participation in consultation breaks this isolation and provides, at the minimum, some release for accumulated tension. At best, consultation provides incentive and insight which leads to the replacement of self-defeating behavior with socially approved and rewarding behavior.

The School and the Family

It is difficult to show how families do and might function and how various sciences contribute to knowledge of the nature and function of families. The difficulty resides in the fact that the anthropological, sociological, and psychological aspects all fuse together in actual life. Hence, the things we would regard as psychological are found to be quite pertinent in sociology. Discussion of the home and family is in a somewhat similar dilemma as regards traditional educational concepts. There are some things commonly regarded as the province of the home over which the school should exercise a "hands off" policy; e.g., sex education. Similarly, there are some things which are responsibilities of the school in which parents should not interfere; e.g., teaching the new mathematics. This, of course, is not how things work in actual practice.

The whole concept of family consultation and family group consultation is based on the premise that *the work of the home and school are inseparable*. Both are concerned with the directed learning processes of the child. When the family is inadequate, when its functions are not performed, when it causes confusion for the child, when the child is so disturbed that he cannot function in school, then these things become a matter of concern to school personnel. It is no more excusable for the school to sidestep the effects of inadequate learning models in the family than it is to ignore slow learners, partially sighted children, or cerebral-palsied individuals by saying that these are medical problems. The child so incapable of living with others that he cannot attend to his school lessons will not be substantially helped by attempts to alleviate symptoms. It is postulated here that the place to attack the problem is in the setting where it occurs. No official dictum and no traditional orientation can alter the need. Arbuckle (1962), discussing the issue of whether or not the school counselor should be a "therapist," concludes that if the child has not been committed to an institution or if he is still in school, he deserves all the help the counselor can give whether it is called "therapy," "teaching," or "personal counseling." Consideration of the individual and his needs precedes the teaching of subject matter simply because the child cannot use his intellect until his emotions are under some degree of control. In a similar vein, it is maintained that if family dysfunction interferes with, or blocks, the traditional function of the school, then — especially in the absence of some other agency's function — school personnel are justified in attempting to establish some liaison. Family consultation, the description of which is the major burden of this monograph, was originally begun with this orientation. Briefly stated, the premise is that (1) some families in contemporary society frequently fail to establish the milieu for building stable personalities, (2) unstable personalities produce, in a few more years, another inadequate family. Thus, a self-perpetuating and self-defeating system is established and maintained.

Both the school and the family are powerful sources of influence on the development of the child. But the family is primary and the school frequently is powerless in competition with any family — adequate or inadequate. Children in school may have many difficulties with learning which can be handled without involving the family. However, the entire learning enterprise improves if the family is a partner with the school in actively seeking to improve the learning environment for the child. A family can respond as readily to positive help as it can defend against attack. Open, mutual concern helps the school, the family, or any institution interested in helping the society achieve success in the development of adequate and productive individuals (Bower, 1965).

One criterion for the success of a family is related to the amount of help required from "outsiders." The genesis of this idea comes from rugged individualism, a British heritage, not from frontier America where every family helped every other family in a kind of cooperation distinctly American. Mutual support was, and is, the "American Way."

Successful families have elaborate and sophisticated behavior that keeps mutual support central to their survival functions. They maintain and sustain one another and share in the support structure of the society to bring about a kind of self-fulfilling prophecy for those who have access to other families (society).

Many families in trouble, however, and particularly those in contemporary industrial and urban America, remain apart and have not acquired knowledge or skills in gaining access to "others." Their difficulties, because of symptoms of aggression, suspicion, and hostility, tend to isolate them and to remain as continuous sources of alienation. Many parents are still practicing pre-urban and pre-industrial behaviors in interpersonal relations, but their children are living in another milieu. The whole family needs confirmation of identity, and this cannot be achieved apart from others, or shall we say, in the isolation which difficulty tends to produce. Knowledge of standards and expectations must come from social contact and social participation — a point at which a family group consultation is of particular value.

Change is a constant phenomenon in all cultures. Learning is a process of change. The attitudes which help one enjoy and accept change cannot be developed in a social vacuum. One must have access to other persons. This is especially true when the rate of change is rapid. Gaining such access requires a complex set of skills. These skills, however, can be experienced *within a family* over a period of years or they can be experienced in a controlled environment within a period of weeks or months. There is probably little concern about the advisability of providing such a controlled environment; the question is whether or not it should be provided by the school. The simple fact is that the family consultation arose and continues to develop from the attempt to help pupils with school problems. A continuing problem in family consultation, as in most helping relationship work, is management of the threat perceived by the cared-for and the caring-for persons. Threat is the discrepancy, perceived by the individual, between the expectations for his performance and his evaluation of behavior (performance). If individuals are motivated by satisfactions from previous experiences (the matching of performance and expectation), productive acting-out behavior usually follows in sequence. However, dissatisfaction with previous experiences may produce bizarre or exotic acting-out behavior (Kluckhohn, 1959). There is the "nothingness" or "no-action" alternative sometimes labeled neutral or withdrawal behavior. The problem is confronted in family consultation by using the "group" method. The access to new or different models of acting-out behavior modifies the conduct of individual family members when exposed to the new experiences over a period of time. The dynamics and forces accountable for the modification of behavior by the group method are discussed by Lewin and Grabbe (1945).

Modification of behavior expressed as a change in conduct requires a change in values by the individual. Such a break with past performance requires an effort equal in magnitude to that encountered whenever a person changes from one culture to another. Cognitive change by acquisition of new knowledge is not sufficient to modify conduct. To learn *about* family consultation is not enough to change conduct. Each of us must become involved — directly — in a group of people. There must be counselors — two or more — and a family or families, one, two, or three. Over a period of six to twelve weeks, the behavior modification of *each* individual will become apparent. The counselors will learn at the same time that family members will learn, although their learning will be individualized in nature, content, and values. Such is the process we call *sharing*. The process is similar to frontier families helping each other. Mutual support of membership in a social group is a central principle of the "American Way" mentioned above. It becomes the role of the counselor to help family members reestablish closer and more active contact with others.

At least some of the difficulty encountered in family consultation stems from behavior that is simply different. Adults seem to be able to cope with the consequences of behavior; but children, it seems, have not been so successful. The parents, upon observing the difficulties experienced by their youngsters, fail to deal adequately with their children or with their peers and classmates. They often become sufficiently aroused to seek the aid proffered by family consultation. Contact with those who are closer to the normal range of behavior, at least in some particular phase of living, seems to have beneficial results. Moreover, it is surprising and gratifying to see that families, who are themselves making errors, are, nevertheless, quite able to see clearly the mistakes of others. It is to help the deviating and self-defeating individuals and families to gain new perspectives that family consultation was devised. Its improvement will continue to rest on the data that anthropologists, sociologists, psychologists, and educators assemble and collate.

3

....

Family Message Systems

It has been shown, in the chapter dealing with multi-disciplines description, that the family is an extremely complex human unit and institution. The satisfaction of many personal and social needs are sought in the family. Many goals are pursued. If the satisfactions sought by one member conflict with those sought by another, misunderstandings invariably result. If the goals pursued are different, unanimity becomes impossible and suspicions and hostilities are likely to arise. Improved communication will not resolve all of the problems of either healthy or unhealthy families, but can minimize some of them. Gaps in knowledge, differential experience, variant attitudes, and personal goals can be narrowed through communication. But let it be admitted that sometimes the gaps are too great, and divorce and separation afford the only relief for members. It is to be hoped such situations are rare. The vehicle for improved family living is improved communication of more personally meaningful messages.

Family consultation may become a concern of school counselors if pupils are involved. There is little discussion herein of "couples counseling." Yet, a couple (man and wife) can serve to show how important consultation and aid in communication can become. Upon the performance of the marriage ceremony, each person is asked to adopt a completely new role. Each must become a responsible and independent adult rather than continuing to act as an irresponsible and dependent child. One needs to cease being the executor of orders and to start initiating action and providing directional orientation. One, as a marriage partner, makes decisions, while when he was a child, the final decision for family action was (at least conventionally) a parental role. Normally one does not marry to get a son or father or daughter or mother — yet this often is the result. Difficulties frequently arise because one of the spouses does not want, or is unable to give up, the role of son or daughter and become a peer and marriage partner. Difficulties may arise because aims, even though discussed, are not shared. One does not readily admit that the aim of marriage is to have legal access to sex relations, or to achieve prestige, or to be provided for financially. These are the hidden motives which, when bared in family consultation, become the beginning point for the new learnings which are basic to satisfactory marriage.

It seems so simple for a young couple to talk — prior to marriage. And it is — at a cognitive level. Cliches gloss over the "feelings" level. During the courtship stage, one may avoid the deeply personal because of (1) lack of skill, and (2) the need to preserve autonomy. But the hidden motives and desires begin to be a cause of emotional festering ("I want children; he doesn't," "I need money for school; she wants new furniture and clothes," etc.), and communication becomes difficult. It is difficult because feelings — intense feelings — are present and, when one expresses them, the other says "You should not feel that way" or "You have no reason to feel that way." But feelings are not dissipated with these reassuring-hostile words. Oddly enough, the *presence* of a third person, even without his active participation, causes a person to describe his feelings differently. One may calmly say, "I want to go to school and all she wants is clothes," while in the counseling session. At home, these words are screamed at a high pitch and adorned with a few expletives.

The non-verbal also becomes a part of the communicating process. The husband may not say, "Honey, I love you," but his prompt return from work, weekends spent at home, his approval of her shopping trips show his love. On the other hand, he may say "Honey, I love you," but not help with the dishes, forget her birthday, and not listen to her complaints about the noisiness in the apartment next door. Communicating in these instances is difficult because of personal emotional involvement. The counselor can be of aid because he knows that there is an affective level to verbal and non-verbal communication that is more important than either word or gesture. These matters will be examined more carefully in the remainder of this section.

Exchange of Meanings

Family consultation is like every other interpersonal process in one dimension: the exchange of personal meanings, one person to another person and among the members of a group of persons. Family *group* consultation provides for many more meanings to be shared and is therefore a more productive model for practice than is a single family. The single family may have only *one way* of interacting, saying things, thinking, or one set of knowledge, traditions, meanings. Another family brings another pattern or model to help members of the single family learn new alternatives for expression of their personal meanings.

The person, as a social unit, may choose from several possible patterns of behavior* to express his own meanings. The range of choice seems to be limited by experience and by emotional condition. If a person is emotionally well controlled, he may be able to gain access to many more of the alternatives to expression in his behavior repertory than if he is fearful or anxiety-laden. The healthy individual can survive massive stress. The emotionally disturbed person can tolerate only limited stress in most situations. These concerns remain with us in family consultation because the meanings communicated in the family message system are the central core.

The mirror of life is represented by a report of what happened to "me." Cultural standards exist to guide us. Family members will tell us what the culture says they *should* report. Counselors search the report for its personal meaning. If three people shared the life event, then, how well do the three *reports* represent common and congruent personal meanings. Note that the emphasis is upon *meanings*, not upon the *content* of the report. "I experience things, life events, other people, etc., in terms of my own personal meanings, not in any *objective* way."

Improvement of communcation is a frequently verbalized goal for counseling. We have found that communication always exists. It is what is, or is not, communicated that either *enhances* or *limits* someone — the sender or the receiver or receivers. What is communicated is not always what the person sending the message thinks and hopes he is communicating; e.g., a father highy anxious about his attractive daughter's welfare, may convey the message that he dislikes and mistrusts her, instead of sincere concern. We focus upon the meanings.† For

---

* A pattern of behavior is used to explain the sequence of life events over a period of time (more than the immediate situation and up to several years). Patterns represent the person as human being and identify him to other persons.

† Whenever a behavior fails to communicate the desired meaning, we say that the sender is engaged in "self-defeating behavior." It has something to communicate but limits in some way what happens next in the sequence of interaction.

FIGURE 1
A Paradigm of Personal Meaning

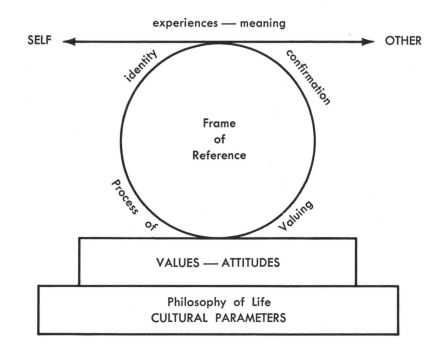

The message system links the person's <u>meaning</u> and <u>identity</u> as SOME-BODY, to events, other people, things, knowledge, and experiences.

example, how do the partners in a marriage renew the contract to stay together? Verbal and non-verbal and non-contextual behavior play important roles. Do the persons include each other when expressing their opinions? How does the "other" person appear (in a good light, poor light, advantaged, disadvantaged)?

Levels of Discourse

Discourse refers to the content of what is said by the person. Levels of discourse extend from one through five, as shown in Figure 2. Begin-

FIGURE 2
Levels of Discourse

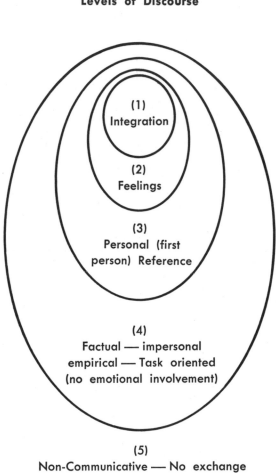

(1)
Integration

(2)
Feelings

(3)
Personal (first
person) Reference

(4)
Factual — impersonal
empirical — Task oriented
(no emotional involvement)

(5)
Non-Communicative — No exchange
of messages (action-reaction)

According to Butler (1966) the counseling process must gain access to levels *three* and *two* if any individual person can hope to move toward *one,* or integration of new behavior into an existing repertoire. Four is an exercise. Five is nothingness.

ning at the center of the circle, the core is labeled *integration*. Here the person achieves an understanding of his feelings and his concerns and creates meaningful relationships resulting in identity for himself in relation to his environmental conditions.

Level two is labeled *feelings*. The person reveals his feelings and his reactions to actual life situations in a way that can be verified against the behaviors observed by the other persons in a group. An individual counselor may do a similar thing with a counselee. The congruence between reported feelings and behavior representation as observed by another person is the validation process used in the confirmation of level two. The key notion is that a person is talking about himself in relation to other persons in an interpersonal relationship situation.

Level three is labeled *personal*. The person talks about his own life situation and begins to use first-person references, including others only occasionally. The counseling process begins at this level. Level three is the beginning of a person's discussion of internal, significant meanings as differentiated from external meanings characterized at level four.

Level four is labeled *factual*. The person faces basic facts. Facts are external things. The distance from the individual is maintained by standing off and making assumptions characteristic of an individual whose concerns are really centered in the management of persons (and things.) The characteristic factor of level four is the lack of any emotional involvement on the part of the individual person. Level four behavior is characterized by the term "cold fish."

Level five is labeled *non-communication*. The person does not show any interest in moving toward considering changing his behavior. The individual may sit quietly in a state of disorganized thought. Such an individual would deny the reality that any discourse is expected. There may be little relationship of one topic to another in his flow of conversation if and when he speaks. Nothing happens in the realm of behavior change when the discourse is conducted at level five. (Fullmer and Bernard, 1966, Butler, 1963).

Double-bind Meanings

The concept of double-bind in the message system of a family comes with communication that has multiple-levels of meanings — and the meanings are somehow contradictory or incongruent. Level one may be the spoken word, or simply what is said. Level two is the qualification of what is said and establishes the contradiction. The symbiotic relationship of a mother and her son will contain many double-bind

messages because she must verbally acknowledge the expected behavior (the cultural norm), but somehow prevent the spoken message
from being implemented. An example of the double-bind may occur
in the qualification of what is said by *affirming* the content but denying
the meaning by making the communication into a joke. A wife and
mother said: "My husband is a wonderful man, but I wish he would
spend less time with his mother. Oh, well, I'm not much good. He is
a wonderful husband" — followed by laughter. The qualification of the
meaning is almost always non-verbal or non-contextual, something like
what a linguist would refer to as super-ordinate-signaling or meaning.
Quote — "I want my son to be normal." But he has no other contact
with any other person than his mother! Mother is the sole, but extremely incomplete, socialization influence. Inadequate socialization
is the cause that disables the youngster. His inability to differentiate
himself from the other person(s) in his environment is the means we
use to understand what is happening. Bateson, et al. (1956), and
Haley (1959) support the idea that such a youngster never learns how
to establish stable alliances with other persons.

Double-bind type messages are frequently passed between parents
and children. The degree of disorganization that results varies, but the
effect is often profound. Even minor conflicting messages can result in
disturbed relationships within the family. Family leadership may be
enhanced or diminished by this dimension of communication. Family
alliances, already mentioned above, can be similarly influenced. Family
interpersonal contracts are influenced because these depend upon establishing a relationship with another person and maintaining such
relationships over extended periods of time. A simple key is available
to test the way a family handles some or all areas of concern. It is the
way a family handles arguments. If a family is not safe enough to
argue, because the risks would be too great, one is dealing with a condition characterized by considerable uncertainty. The counselor should
look closely at anything a family *omits* from its behavior pattern. It
may mean they have not learned some skills or knowledge which family
consultation might teach. It may be even more complicated. The
counselor's task is to learn to read and comprehend the family folklore.

Family Folklore

Every family has a folklore. It is the story each member of a family
will tell, if asked. It is my *family's* story, not just *my* story! Folklore
represents the family and its intra-family communication or message
system. Family folklore is an elaborate message system. The linguist
might refer to this phenomenon as a story told by using a restrictive

code. Each member has his feeling of mutual support and safety needs met by being *in* the family. Each member can *expect* his demands to be met.

One way of looking at a family member who is acting-out is to see him as apart *from* rather than a part *of* a family. The identified problem child is challenging the system in some way and for some very personal reasons. The counselors, in family consultation, *must* learn to "read" the family message folklore. Examples would require complete case reports, but perhaps the potential "reader" could be aided by some anecdotes. A family always has some private myth, such as "everyone in our family was a good student." In such a family, the youngster having difficulty in achievement in school will be in a bind or conflict. "I always say that every one *ought to be* law abiding — or neat — or friendly — or helpful — or whatever." (There is usually little confirming evidence to validate that such a person ever *really* does what he says.) The saying or repeating of the myth (or private meaning) is seen somehow by the person as enough. We see it as a kind of *denial* when verbal behavior is substituted for acting-out behavior.

Inter-family Communication

A family has a system for sending messages to other families, institutions, and individuals. Consultation is a process that requires counselors to understand at least three very specific aspects of the inter-family message system utilized by each family in family group consultation. It is no less significant for single family units in consultation.
1. What message(s) can be shared? Can a message be sent or received? Under what conditions can sharing occur? What antecedents, ground rules, limits, expectations, and reasons are used to regulate the message sharing?
2. What meaning(s) is shared?
   There are two major dimensions:
   a. The meaning that permits a message to be shared.
   b. The meaning that is denied or left-out — omitted — cannot be shared.
3. What is the interaction pattern that is used to transfer messages?
   a. One person to another
   b. One person to the group
   c. The group to one or more persons

Examples are complex, because we are talking of *patterns of behavior* rather than labels or isolated incidents. An entire experience with a family or group of families is necessary to explain the message-systems idea to a counselor. We do it in direct experience with supervised practice. In the beginning, we had to start by actually working with families in a consultation setting. Then patterns began to emerge. In dialogue with other counselors, the patterns began to evolve meanings we could share. A way of talking about family consultation has developed. You, the reader, are coming into the midst of an on-going conversation. The antecedents are obscure because you haven't experienced what is being discussed. We suggest you get some experience. Invite a family to join you in trying to find ways of helping one youngster. Use your common sense and live through five or six sessions spaced in time over about 2 months. Invite a second, and possibly a third, counselor to sit in with you for the demonstration. The behavior forces you will be utilizing are all "natural" to our culture. If you can live with your anxiety (shared with one or two colleagues) for a few weeks, the payoff will be more understanding of what it is that we are talking about. Without the direct encounter with a family over a period of weeks, our statements are like so much *folklore*. A word of caution: Each person usually has experience in his own family. We each have our own message systems. *Do not misread someone's meanings by interpreting their messages using your system.* There is more to the caution than just listening. I am unable to understand someone else until I can comprehend the other person's meaning. The first person is used to emphasize the central idea (Loban, 1966).

A Way of Thinking

The cognitive process employed by a family is usually quite closely related to similar processes in other families within a given culture. The major concern with the way a family thinks is related to whether the members are able to use rational processes or whether they have learned some irrational processes (Friedman, 1965). The counselor is the only source of judgment in this evaluation. Judgment is a necessary step in delineating the areas in which a family may be entirely rational in the way they think about their concerns and their problems in living. However, a family may have learned irrational ways of thinking and may continuously reap a rather negative harvest from the output of this kind of process (self-defeating behavior, see Fullmer and Bernard, 1964).

How a family thinks has a direct bearing upon what a family can do about those immediate and long term conditions to which they must respond. In other words, a family is limited to one alternative as a way of thinking. This condition limits the choices of alternatives in other areas. Once a family has made a choice of alternatives, it is restricted in the subsequent choices, or one might say, it is committed to a course or direction. The consequence of change would be chaos, and might have a disorganizing effect upon the operation (personality) of the family. The way of thinking utilized by the family has a direct bearing upon the level of integration of the family in its relationships, one to another, and its relationships to outside forces, persons, and conditions. Loban (1966) tells us how to recognize the thinking pattern of a family. The usage of language represents a way of thinking and levels of thinking. The expansion of a sentence from the basic, "Billy cried," to read "Billy cried because he was very upset over the neighbor boy's expansive attitude toward their joint contributions to the Scout program to raise funds for the summer camp." The amplification of verbal communication from basic patterns like "Billy cried" brings out many more interdependent relationships. Understanding the way a family thinks or individual family members think helps the counselors comprehend the level of thinking. The ramifications help a counselor relate *his* meanings to the meanings within a family. Meaningful action can be taken by the counselors. If asked, "How did you know to do what you just did do?" I am able to explain the signals I read, the meanings interpreted, in a way that helps the questioner learn to do the same kind of signal reading.

There is a considerable void in the literature about families and family patterns concerning the way a healthy family thinks. There is a literature based upon families in trouble or families suffering from some psychopathology. It is difficult to generalize from the disturbed or sick family to the healthy family. We do not know whether there is any similarity between the sick family and the healthy family on any of the interpersonal dimensions. We encounter a family able to amplify sentences, but one of its youngsters is in difficulty. We then need to establish whether certain topics and conditions can be discussed. From such information, we make inferences about the family's ability to think. There seems to be little congruence among the ability to use language, ability to think, and the frequency of disturbed behavior by one or more family members. We examine the restrictions a family places around the things it seems able to think about and the things it avoids. The healthy family seems able to think about almost anything that comes along, or needs its attention. The family in difficulty is a family that may have several taboos operating to control the degree of involvement possible for any member of the family, or the family as a group, concerning thinking about certain topics, areas, or conditions. The family may practice a kind of escape to high level verbal abstraction, while continuing to maintain a destructive emotional climate.

The incidence of agreement is less important than the level of functioning within a family. The healthy family is able to function with real solidarity whenever it is necessary. Strong feelings resulting from disagreement between or among family members do not generalize

to all other areas and incapacitate the family unit. The family in
trouble usually is incapacitated in *all* areas until the conflict(s) is/are
resolved. The conventional wisdom in our culture, that "one should
learn to live with his problems," seems to have relevance for the idea
under discussion. The healthy family uses conflict to establish learning
experiences. The family in trouble seems to be disabled by conflict.
This is an observable difference and can be used by counselors to
differentiate healthy from disturbed families. The inadequate family
tends to isolate itself and thus reduce the possibility of encountering
adequate models.

Friedman, et al. (1965), has used a family participation index and a
disagreement scale to study families of schizophrenics. For families
in trouble, these evaluative devices seem relevant. For healthy families, we question the validity of such devices. The healthy family lives
productively with many conflicts, incongruities, and discrepancies,
without charging any one of its members too high a price. In fact,
there seems to be an increase in ability to tolerate stress in healthy
families in direct proportion to conflict conditions. Research is necessary to test these assumptions. We would caution generalizing from
sick families to healthy families because they seem to be different *kinds*
of units or entities.

A family seems to be more inhibited in what it thinks *about* than
what it thinks *of.* The reason why a family cannot think about something may be hidden among complex attitudes at deep emotional commitment levels. In other words, our knowledge only goes so far.
Because the family can think *about* a condition, it does not necessarily
resolve its dilemmas and conflict. But, on the other hand, if a family
is restricted *from* thinking, it is certain that there can be little hope for
resolution. Until some research has been systematically carried out to
test the comparisons between *sick* and *healthy* families, it is unlikely
that anyone will get beyond opinion or speculation, except insofar as
one describes empirical experiences in working with families over long
periods of time. There are some very difficult research problems involved in matching families because of the nature of the autonomy
given to a family unit in the American form of Western-European culture. Mobility and autonomy from any kinship pattern beyond the
immediate father-mother-household is only one facet of this basic
problem.

Parents derive their ways of thinking from growing up in a family
with their own parents. This pattern is continued in the presence of
their own children, who also learn. When we look at how family members think, we are looking at the thought processes and the knowledge
system used by the family. The pattern may reach across two or more

generations. Social mobility may complicate the nature and scope of the impact of new knowledge from other social class levels. Geography is also a factor in social mobility; e.g., rural vs urban residence.

The thought processes are concerned with the kinds of logic and the way of reasoning utilized by the family. The way of thinking about something is based upon a set of assumptions, usually not verbalized, and a set of principles and corollaries that serve the purpose of metering into and out of the individual's system of thinking those elements that are congruent with his basic purposes, perceived by him to add to the possibility of enhancing his situation. There are games that can be used to assist individuals to learn how they use their thought processes. One of these is the kind of game that gives you a set of limits and a problem that you cannot solve unless you step outside of the limits and restructure the possibilities from a different vantage point. A thought process is a mental set or psychological set that an individual maintains. We see this in family consultation in the form of the *repeated question.* The mother may ask the same question again and again, and again, although it is apparent to the counselor(s) that the repeated question will not increase her ability to comprehend what is happening anymore than she has so far. It is not possible to help her understand why she should ask any *other* question. Thus, she will continue to ask the same question. "But why does Junior persist in behaving this way?" or "Why doesn't he (husband) plant grass in our yard?" Such a message may be carried by an infinite variety of wordings for questions, but, basically, the mother is asking questions that represent a way of thinking about Junior or husband and what is happening. Her way of thinking has set a limit to what she can possibly comprehend at the moment. The task in family consultation is to help the mother expand the horizon of her possibilities for understanding the situation in which she is engaged.

Message systems used by families constitute a collection of skills and common wisdoms that have been passed along from one generation to another. These have been modified and added to as new experiences were achieved by individual members and incorporated into the family structure and education. Education is the universal modifier and equalizer of knowledge available to people within our culture. The basic principle that we concern ourselves with in family consultation is as follows: *Change and learning* are synonymous concepts.

Almost all people will resist change because it requires a restructuring and a realignment of most of the contracts and alliances an individual has achieved with other significant persons. If learning is perceived as change, then learning probably will be resisted (Lewin and Grabbe, 1945). Our experiences in working with families in consultation seem to confirm this principle although systematic study would be required to validate such an assumption. The reader is cautioned to regard the assumption as unverified. Assuming that most people will resist change and therefore will resist learning, it is necessary to assume further that each counselor will be dealing with *reluctant learners* when he works with families in consultation.

Another principle we have found that seems to be supported by our experiences with families is: *A family uses everything it knows, all of the time.* A corollary to this principle is, that those things the family does not know represent either knowledge voids, experience voids, or taboos about which the family consultation sessions may revolve. A curious factor encountered in family consultation is the circuitous aspect of a family as it attempts to utilize all of its knowledge and skills to steer the counselors around and through their maze of "unknowns." The "unknowns" are, at first appearance, sometimes experienced as *secrets*. However, on further investigation many of these so-called *secrets* are actually *voids*. Voids are gaps in knowledge systems. It is a well-known fact that class and cultural differences consist mainly of different kinds and amounts of knowledge about life and life events, and the sequence and priorities by which lives are managed. A family within one social class, or a mobile family moving from one social class to another, may, in the process of one or two generations, acquire much of the knowledge of a second social class while retaining certain taboos or knowledge voids apparent in the previous social class. The literature on psychology deals with this condition in an individual as certain kinds of neuroticism and certain kinds of fixations and/or conscious-unconscious motivations. It is not yet clear to us exactly how it could be described in a family, but the behavior experienced in family consultation leads us to speculate that a family is aware, only vaguely, that they do not know something. Family members may discover an important *idea*. If they can identify what it is they do not know, and if they can achieve the attitude that they want to learn about what they do not know, it is possible for family members to begin to change behavior. Further, the possibilities arise for rather rapid change or learning if the counselors (who are consulting with them and the other families who are in the group) can contribute directly to the information or knowledge voids. The changed behavior even appears sometimes as a kind of sudden health or sudden change in the whole climate, attitudinal climate, and/or psychological climate of the family. Schofield (1966) has called this the process of helping parents develop as persons so that they can become more adequate as mothers and fathers.

An example might be helpful. A family had a thirteen-year-old boy who was acting-out in a very manipulative way and controlling the family. Both parents and siblings were controlled by getting them into the position where they would attempt to appease the thirteen-year-old. In the appeasement process, the family was attempting a kind of double-bind meaning, saying, "Ah, come on, be like the culture," and laughing or making a joke of what they were trying to do. The meaning for the thirteen-year-old youngster seemed to be that he was being rewarded for his controlling behavior. It was a self-defeating pattern because he never really achieved any membership status within the family. Indeed, the family was helped to verbalize their understanding of whether or not it was a real meaning that this youngster really didn't have a place in the family. He was an "outsider." A very marked change in the psychological climate of this family was achieved following one session in which the counselors demonstrated the method by which the youngster manipulated the parents and his siblings. Once this was revealed, the parents changed their whole attitudinal climate toward *their own behavior* and consequently the boy's behavior. In short, they no longer responded like puppets to the controlling behavior of the boy. It could be stated as a *change* in behavior or it could be said that the parents *learned* to be effective, rather than ineffective, in their response pattern with the son. With a few follow-up sessions, it was possible to terminate consultation and the family was able to move ahead on its own.

It can be seen that the knowledge system of a family is closely attuned to the thought processes a family can utilize, and sets many limits around how a family *thinks.* How a family thinks circumscribes what it allows into its perceptual field. A feeling of adequacy is difficult to maintain in the presence of too much ambiguity. "I may perceive the *need to learn* as showing loss of face as a parent." We counselors handle this one by learning *with* the family!

Things

Things represent prestige, rituals, and meanings to a family. A family can send many messages to the rest of the world by the kinds of *things* it acquires. Meanings, emanating from the individual members of a family or the family as a group, can be transferred to other persons in other families and to the world in general. These meanings are expressed through the way in which *things* are used by the family. Hall (1959) talks about the way things are used under the primary message system called *exploitation.* How we use *things* reveals much about our regard for other persons. Our use or exploitation of our environment can be destructive or enhancing. It depends on what message we are sending.

Traditions

Traditions are roles in our society for individuals and institutions. The father role, the mother role, the role of the oldest sibling, the middle sibling, and the youngest sibling, the sister sibling and the brother sibling, the aunts, the uncles, and other kinship pattern personalities represent the concepts that traditions, and the message systems therein, refer to in a family, a church, a school.

Counselors need to learn early in the consultation session how to read the meanings used by the family in its traditions. The counselors can see the role models provided for children by parents and other significant persons. From the observations, it is possible to gain more understanding of family process — the sharing of meanings through role identification and role modeling.

Families in difficulty may have examples of negative role-models. A parent may be an anti-model for one of the youngsters. An anti-model may be the parent who rejects one child, while responding positively to a second child. The overprotecting-parent is another common example. Family consultation may not be sufficient to help resolve the anti-model condition. We have not experienced much success with this condition.

The entire purpose of looking at message systems within the family is to attempt to get a way of systematically describing what happens between the counselors and the family members in family consultation.

The events of communication represent the basic target for description in the message system as described above.

The transfer of culture from parent to child is a crucial function of tradition or parental roles. The process is provided within the learning model of a healthy family. When something hinders the healthy process, the family usually experiences difficulty.

The basic principle is: the roles or traditions provided within a healthy family produce individual stability within the group. If the roles are sustained over long periods of time, the learning person confirms himself and his process for learning. The value or payoff comes because the person can reproduce the role and the life situation under *new* conditions at a later time.

Such is the impact of the bio-social unit (family) for survival of human behavior. Human behavior must be learned. Only lower animals *inherit* behavior. Getting a look at the human learning process is very difficult because each of us is a participant. We must, self-consciously and systematically, learn to observe the phenomena. In family consultation, we do our learning in counselor-pairs or teams so that a check-and-balance system of supervision is always available. We need to demand a check on our participant-observer behavior.

Touching

Symbolic meanings *touch* our lives every day. Normal persons have access to others for touching and for being touched — every day. Make a check list of whom you touch, how many times, when, where (both anatomically and geographically), and note who it is you manage to have touch you, similarly. This may be more revealing than verbal facts. The taboos surrounding "touching" are in the culture. There is a common wisdom in the cliche, "It was a touching scene." This can be any scene, e.g., a mother's initial embrace of her soldier son coming home from the war, two lovers (implies they are in each other's arms) sending messages to each other. The greeting between any two persons carries a message. Verbal confirmation is simply a ritual. There is a language of the skin.

Self-consciousness must be included when discussing any "touching" scene. Counselors can learn much of significance from observing a family before, during, and following a consultation session. Watch, especially, who touches whom, under what conditions, and be alert to catch any symbolic touching, e.g., a gesture of extending an arm toward the other person, or directing a glance sometimes made more emphatic by a nod of the head.

Children learn to interpret a wide range of subtle "touching" symbols. The easiest way to disenfranchize oneself from a group of children in a classroom is to begin acting without due regard for what one's gestures, intonations, and word-sequences mean to the youngsters. Children from different social classes have private meanings for what the teacher does and says. The teacher usually learns to clarify and create a common language (meanings) with her youngsters. (These restricted codes are most frequently formed between a teacher and each youngster. The counselor can observe this by listening to the teacher describe the youngsters with whom she has established *contact* and those that seem to remain beyond her reach.) Family consultation provides many more opportunities if counselors observe the parental pattern of touching a youngster and relate it to the teacher's pattern.

The messages transmitted by physical, figurative, and symbolic "touching" have profound consequences for each person. Like the simple fact that behind every bribe-taker is a bribe-giver, the counselor should *learn* to read both parts of the message — similar to Mortimer, who experienced difficulty with reading in school: He didn't know if he should read the white or the black. The reader is frequently asked to read between the lines!

Family consultation brings a complicated mass of communications to unravel. The counselors should be able to confirm the *real message(s)* exchanged within a family by comparing the non-verbal "touching" behavior, and meanings may be infinite. The task of detailing enough specifics to help the reader to any significant degree would require a substantial volume. It may be helpful to note that a counselor can begin systematically to observe himself and other people in the act of "touching." Believe what is seen because the meanings are basic. Everyone needs contact with someone else. It is a productive source of knowledge about life in a family. "Farewell, stay in contact, keep in touch!"

4

Family Consultation:
History, Method, and Procedure

The healthy family is one of the most effective learning models available in Western culture. Family consultation attempts to improve the efficiency and efficacy of the family learning model. One of the direct impacts of family consultation is aimed at the problem of learning-how-to-learn. The process of making conscious the business of learning and comprehending is the major emphasis.

In attempting any work with a family, it is essential that the integrity of the family group be maintained at all times, whether they are being seen as an individual family, or whether they are being seen in the company of other families in family group consultation.

The question of who should be *in* and/or *out* of family group consultation, or any other form of counseling or helping relationships work, is an open question. We are biased toward the view that all families can learn in direct proportion to the experiences they can command, including opportunity to encounter other families in a learning environment. Access to other persons and families is the major contribution to the educational setting and the school's responsibility for helping the youth grow into maturity. We would favor allowing a family which desires family consultation to be given the opportunity of at least six or eight sessions, just to learn the *methods* by which learning-how-to-learn and comprehending becomes a conscious process.

Family consultation began as an effort to find a more productive model for working in schools with youngsters identified as learning and/or behavior problems. More than five years have been devoted to the development of systematic empirical studies and research on the method. The work setting for family consultation includes family units and groups of family units. Such groups working together on problems are called family group consultation. Up to four families may be involved in a consultation setting. In addition to the group of family units, a single family unit may be seen in consultation. One-to-one sessions for individual family members are held as well as small group sessions for individual family members involving individuals from within family units and from different family units. More than one family unit may be used to provide individuals for a peer group, reference group, and small counseling group sessions.*

The History of Family Consultation

Family consultation was begun more than five years ago at the Out-patient Clinic of the University of Oregon Medical School. The psychiatrist in charge of the Outpatient Clinic, John L. Butler, M.D., gave medical supervision to the initial group of families referred from the Medical School Outpatient Psychiatric Clinic. The method of family consultation was started in response to the need for working with youngsters referred through social agencies from the school to the Medical School Outpatient Clinic for diagnosis and treatment of learning and/or behavior disorders at home and at school. There was no pathology identified by the psychiatrists in any of the youngsters. However, teacher reports included mild to incorrigible acting-out behavior disorders. Also, considerable difficulty, labeled underrealization of academic potential, was found in achievement test scores compared with intelligence test scores recorded by the schools. It was felt that, if a successful method of working with the family, the youngsters, and teachers could be developed, school counselors could apply such a method in the educational setting with the goal of reducing the incidence of incorrigibility and increasing appropriate achievement of individual youngsters in relation to academic potential.

After the initial year of supervised practice, the original group of families was moved to the human relations laboratory of the Division of Continuing Education. Continued development and application of

---

* It may be helpful to indicate at this point, as will be explained later in some detail, that family consultation and family group consultation involve two or more counselors. One takes the lead with the whole group; typically, the group breaks into child and parent groups, each of which requires at least one leader.

the method has been carried on during the subsequent years. There has been a considerable increase in the numbers of families and groups involved in the continuing consultation sessions. For one month during a recent year, over 700 individual contact sessions (each session lasting from 1½ to 2 hours in length) were carried on in the human relations laboratory under supervision of counseling center staff. Family consultation has become an integral part of a graduate counselor-education program for school counselors. Much of the work is done in the school setting. There have been as many as forty trainees at a time conducting family group consultation as part of their endeavor to learn counseling skills.

Following the initial year of development at the Medical School Psychiatric Outpatient Clinic, the enrollees in a Counseling and Guidance Institute program, under the sponsorship of the National Defense Education Act, conducted family group consultation sessions on a six-weeks terminal arrangement within their laboratory schools. The school response was so positive that subsequent NDEA Institute enrollment groups carried on extended periods of family group consultation within their laboratory school setting.

It should be emphasized that the goals and purposes of the family consultation program are to improve the learning environment for the youngster in the educational setting. Family consultation had its genesis in a psychiatric clinic. However, the method was not devised to be used in the medical setting. Rather, the medical setting was inappropriate for the problems referred to it by the persons from the educational setting. This is an extremely important distinction (educational setting vs. medical setting), and it is mentioned because of the confusion that abounds concerning the nature of the methods appropriate to working in each of these settings, respectively. The authors' experience in training has bridged both settings — the educational and the medical. Our experimental work in counseling and our training work continued to carry psychiatric supervision. This has been provided by the same psychiatrists under whom the initial experimental work was done, namely, John L. Butler, M.D., and George Saslow, M.D., University of Oregon Medical School, Portland, Oregon. We have learned to pay attention to the common elements involved in the educational setting and/or the psychiatric setting concerning any methods designed to modify human behavior.

Paradoxically, human behavior may be extremely difficult or disarmingly easy to modify. To change a personality, to change the acting-out behavior pattern of an individual, to construct or influence the modifications of development and growth patterns in an individual human being, are among the most difficult tasks in which one can engage. On the other hand, when changes come, they are so marked that one wonders what one has done, what has happened that such modification could occur so rapidly. It would appear, on some occasions at least, that the change is easy, but that the consolidation of a new habitual pattern of living is somewhat more difficult. At least it is difficult to invest enough time to permit the individual sufficient practice for the behavioral change to become established.

Family consultation continues as a method concerned with behavior modification in a format especially applicable in educational settings. It is particularly useful when practiced by school counselors with children who experience behavior and/or learning difficulties.

The Method of Family Consultation

Entering into a helping relationship with a family system is like entering enemy territory. One should expect to get shot down and to live as a "captive" within a portion of the family domain. Mitchell (1965) describes two conditions that are typical of the defense systems employed by families in trouble to keep the counselor on the periphery.

One defense system consists of an openly threatening stance, such as barricading the front door to the home. (It should be remembered that Mitchell worked with families of schizophrenic patients in their own homes.) The family might seek to make the counseling session into a social occasion rather than a professional work session. A second defense system is the reverse of the first condition; that is, the family may be willing to include the counselor or counselors into an intimate relationship, but subtly obligates them not to change anything, especially the family's operating system of defenses.

These defenses are commonly encountered with families in family group consultation sessions. Indeed, it is our basis for calling the work with families, *consultation,* instead of counseling or therapy. The word *therapy* is not used because of the general concept about its meaning characterized by negative attitudes and some confusion among school personnel.

Saslow (1966) maintains that such a general term as "therapy" is largely undefined except to mean the altering of a person's behavior. Included in the meaning of "therapy" are such terms as "education," "counseling," "guidance," "brainwashing," "totalism," (a highly coercive technique), and any other general term used to describe a relationship between two or more persons when *learning* new behavior is the essence of the encounter. Saslow further suggests educators should look closely at their *ways of saying things.* Much of what is said is so general that it is meaningless. In other circumstances, the meanings are in conflict, i.e., "counselors should not do *therapy*, but, it is all right to help a youngster learn alternative ways of behaving in situation B in order to avoid a destructive consequence of being ejected from situation A."

Procedures in Family Consultation

Intake

Intake procedures (See Chapter 5) for family consultation require meeting(s) of an entire family unit and two or more counselors in a group setting. The counselors should have minimum access to information concerning the family prior to the first meeting. This provides a way of comparing the counselors' accuracy of perception of the family with other observers. This provides some assurance that preconceived notions will not bias the search for confirming evidence or blind the consultant to novel perceptions. Evaluation and confirmation are important concerns in family consultation. These are included in the initial procedures.

During the initial session, a brief history of the family is taken. The family is asked to tell its story concerning its present condition. The family is asked to state what it hopes to achieve from the family consultation sessions. Additionally, each individual family member is asked to express his hopes, aspirations, and feelings about his presence with the family in the consultation session.

Each counselor is expected to explain the role and the purpose of family consultation in relatively simple terms; e.g., the object of family consultation is to help the family learn about its means of communicating with one another so that individuals within the family may achieve a higher level of productivity in whatever area(s) concerns them. A general goal of behavior modification for individuals or the family as a group constitutes the objective outlined for family consultation. It is well not to attempt in-depth analysis of the goals and objectives for family consultation during the *initial* session. It is important to stress the condition of *learning* together as a basic focus of family consultation.

The intake stage extends up to three sessions. Our experience confirms the need for more than one session with intervening time lapses to help the family explore the implications of continuing family group consultation or family consultation.

The extended period of intake time allows counselors and family members to learn the methods of communication that will be employed in the family consultation sessions. It must be determined whether other families will be added to the group to make it family group consultation, or whether the family will be seen as a single unit. The counselors determine how many of the family members will receive individual counseling concurrently with the group consultation or consultation sessions.

The N of One: Focus upon the Individual

It is assumed that human behavior is very difficult to change, but this assumption is qualified by the further assumption that no existing mold of human behavior is necessarily permanent. Systematic study of behavior is possible through counseling (Rogers, 1961). Family consultation has repeatedly confirmed that there is a high level of persistence in the patterns of human behavior found within a family. There does not seem to be any impediment to learning because of chronological age. Family consultation experience has led us to look with favor upon the concept of the "N of 1." The N of 1 is particularly useful as a concept in family consultation because the specific emphasis is upon behavior modification and particularly specified in terms of one individual. The one *person* is the focus for change in behavior. The N of 1 is how we express this.

Another concept found useful in family group consultation and family consultation is that if we are to be understood and if we are to understand others in a family, all participants must *unlearn* certain modes of speaking and listening. Unless a common language with common reference points is learned and spoken within a common frame-of-reference, our understanding and concern may be simply an exercise of sympathy rather than an empathic, productive, learning situation.

The Initial Consultation

In the procedures with family consultation, we must find a place to begin. This is a profound and continuing concern among those who are being introduced to family consultation. If a person wants to improve his performance or if a person has had some bad experiences, the counselor must begin by helping that individual, wherever he is. We begin in family consultation by getting *tuned in* to the other person's message system. This may be visualized as a mode of listening. However, listening by itself is not enough. *It is necessary to share experiences with the other persons until such time as the common mode of expression can be stabilized and confirmed.* The *here and now* orientation of the shared experience is an approach to developing a common language between the counselors and the family members. The difficulties attending a genetic or historical approach to family experience leads to the evolvement of fictions and folklore. Myths and illusions will distort the meaning of what is communicated. We may begin by simply saying, "This is the experience I have had, here-and-now. I am interested in your experiences, here-and-now."

The counselor begins as an expert struggling with the same problem in communication that is experienced by the other family members. In struggling together, the counselor and the family will evolve a set of *common meanings* tied to the experiences they have together in the here-and-now. One must recognize the limits of one's own power to act in the here-and-now. There is a definite limitation upon the power of the counselor to act in any more dynamic and productive ways than those equally available to each member of the family. Likewise, the counselor cannot assume any of the power of the family group. This is the exclusive domain of the family members and will be expressed by the person in the family who holds command or control of the other members. This person is identified in the intake as the "spokesman" for the family. Identification of the family's spokesman is fundamentally and relatively difficult because the family may choose to hide this person through either conscious or unconscious motivation or behavior. Unconscious problems sometimes become conscious to the individual during counseling and consultation. Family consultation seeks to make each individual member of a family conscious of the conditions under which he is living. The choices among possible alternative courses to action (behavior) become possible. Some families choose to continue living with the problems they have. Some families choose change.

The counselors in family consultation sometimes are prone to underestimate the capabilities of the individual members of a family and, indeed, of the family unit itself. In working with families in a consultation or counseling relationship, it is strongly recommended that counselors remain fully aware of this particular problem. When we deal with the family in a consultation session it is necessary to recall the limitations of our own experience and the possibilities of underestimating and/or overestimating our own ability to meet a new situation on the basis of past and present experience.

The Skill of Paraphrasing

In the exchanges between the counselor and the individual family members, it is essential to avoid head-on confrontation, because it yields no gain, i.e., "yes, you did," "no, I didn't," "why did you do this?" or pointing out that mother does have a symbiotic relationship with a son, and other direct no-alternative confrontations. Disagreement always needs a time lapse to modify the meaning it has for each participant. Each individual needs to learn how to *paraphrase* what each other person is saying. Paraphrasing is a means of abstracting the *meaning* in the communication received during the interaction with another person. If I say to you, "I believe that extremist groups are bad for the social system," you would have the choice of open agreement or disagreement, or the choice of clarifying the meaning of what I had said. If you were to say to me, "I disagree with what you have said; I think extremist groups are extremely good for our social system," that would be disagreement. If, however, you were to paraphrase my statement, it might be possible to say, "Are you telling me that you would not support an extremist group?"

Paraphrasing is the simple re-structuring of the content of one person's statement or communication in "my" own words. One may use the form of a question to avoid the *finality* inherent in a direct statement. Paraphrasing helps to clarify meanings and to avoid a direct confrontation based on some implied or covert disagreement. Paraphrasing can be used to avoid disagreements and to explore the irrational attacks that may be made by one person upon another in family consultation. The power of paraphrasing lies in its ability to help find areas that are safe to explore within the family dynamics; i.e., those subjects about which individuals within the family are allowed to talk openly.

Paraphrasing can be used successfully by counselors who are responsible for informal exchanges with PTA groups, teachers, administrators, board of education members, as well as other human behavior specialists within the school setting. It is extremely important to allow sufficient time for informal exchanges because of the payoff in consensus, mutual understanding or clarification of issues, and comprehension by those persons in positions to support or to attack the family consultation program.

Feedback, Listening, Hearing, and Validation

It is extremely important to understand the concept of *feedback*. One of the ways we have found productive is to look at feedback as a system of clarification and evaluation in interpersonal interaction among members of a family, family(s) and counselors, among counselors, and among interested persons and the counselors. Feedback is essential if a counselor is to clarify the meanings that are being exchanged among persons. Impact is a concept closely associated with the concept of feedback. The impact "I" am having upon another person can be assessed only in terms of the "feedback" I get. If I modify* my behavior, I can "read" the changes in behavior "feedback"

---

* What about the quality of "credible behavior" if one has the flexibility to choose among many alternatives to behave (act out) (respond) in a here-and-now interaction with others? I can be versatile if I have more than one choice upon which to act.

from the other person and make an assessment of the impact my behavior is having upon him. The assessment is based upon my ability to observe both verbal and non-verbal message systems in action under the here-and-now conditions of interpersonal interaction.

A way we have used to establish the conditions under which one can learn to "read" the feedback from his behavior in terms of the other person's reaction is to look closely at the nature of comments made about *my* behavior. We begin with the question, "What is happening now?" In order to answer this question, it is necessary for me to say what *I think* is happening now, in terms of what I am doing at this moment. It is necessary for the other individuals to make similar personal statements. The congruence or divergence of the messages in these statements constitutes the point where we *begin* the assessment process of learning whether or not we are reading the situation in a similar or differing way as group members. The value of this procedure resides in the fact that whether we are agreeing or disagreeing makes no difference in whether we can proceed. In other words, most of the confrontation aspects of this kind of interaction are nullified, and the subject is clarification of what is happening rather than reaction and valuing what is happening in terms of some a priori set of criteria that each individual carries with him.

Learning and Teaching

Another way of looking at comments on *my* behavior is to ask whether they are psychological. If they are merely descriptive for testing the meaning that you should attach to *my* behavior or that another person should attach to *my* behavior, they are not necessarily psychological. The possibility of choosing a wide variety of commentary that would not be psychological concerning *my* behavior, or anyone's behavior is always possible.* However, in a family consultation session, it is almost always assumed by the participants that most comments about "my behavior" are psychological. The problem presented by so called "pyschological statements or comments on my behavior," is the over-enamored element of *affect*. Descriptive statements are less likely to exclude the possibility of including cognitive material as part of the learning environment. The counselor-educator is not necessarily a counselor in his interaction with students. Therefore, the counselor-educator should include much cognitive material at those moments in the stream-of-affect (feelings and emotions) that

---

* Youngsters tell us that comments which tend to "rank" or "diagnose" their behavior are very objectionable. "Do not classify me, because it makes me feel like a thing instead of a person." We hear the message not to condescend and not to patronize, but relate as equals.

make the cognitive material most likely to be comprehended. The master teacher is a person who has this ability, whether conscious or unconscious, to meet the most opportune moment in the experience (a sense of timing) with the child for his learning of cognitive material. He includes a high incidence of congruence between the *affect* (the emotional condition of the learner) and the *cognitive* material to be learned.

Performance Anxiety

There is a large element of performance anxiety associated with both the counselor's behavior and the individual family member's behavior in family consultation, because family consultation is not the usual format for meeting with a family in our culture. Because it violates the usual cultural pattern, the individuals will respond to this as being somewhat "unnatural" in their experience. Performance anxiety will very rapidly subside providing the counselor can lead the discussion into the realm of what-is-happening-now in this situation. What is to be expected in this situation? What are the possible responsibilities, alternatives, and outcomes that will benefit each participating individual? The family consultation setting is designed to be both a direct-experience setting for educating counselors as well as for learning by individual family members. *Family consultation is not a discussion about life and living; it is a segment of experience from the total life processes.*

Groups of Two or More Families in Consultation

The family group consultation method is much more productive for the school setting, particularly in terms of helping parents establish new reference groups from whom they can get some kind of reality-testing experience for their own family practices. The opportunity to share meaningful learning experiences with other persons is tremendously limited in modern culture. Access to other families is often very limited for certain classes of families. Families having difficulties with their youngsters are sometimes isolated because they do not feel free to make direct contact with other families. The learning that takes place is partly a learning-to-participate. Shared experience allows a given family opportunities to learn the means by which they can share and learn those things that are necessary for survival.

Individuals within family groups learn to make contacts on their own. Family groups take on behavior modification within each family on their own terms. The family group consultation sessions become a "sounding board" for reporting, evaluating, and confirming the new behaviors that have been attempted on an experimental basis. The sources of these learnings, of course, are other families, the counselors, each other, the school, the church, and other peer group contacts which individuals maintain outside of the family group consultation sessions. Learning from "each other" in the above sentence is especially interesting because in the consultation sessions one so frequently observes and sometimes hears voiced, "I turn him (her) off," "I really wasn't listening." When members begin to listen, they begin to hear *and* subsequently to learn.

Length of Sessions

The length of sessions depends upon the nature of the concern being treated. If the concerns of a family are so severe, and the crisis so immediate, that it requires the attention and concentration of two counselors plus one individual family, then these needs should be accommodated immediately. As a general rule, however, the sequence is as follows:

The families come into a group, meet around a table or in a room filled with chairs in a circle, with the counselors scattered among the families. The meeting proceeds for about forty-five minutes to an hour. The children and the parents of all of the families are present with the counselors. There is a short break after the initial period, and two subgroups are formed. One subgroup consists of the parents and a counselor, and the second subgroup consists of the children and the second counselor. Thus, the need for a minimum of two counselors working as a team is seen. If there is a wide range in the ages of the youngsters, it is advisable to have more than one subgroup of children. We have had as many as three subgroups of children, ranging in age from preschoolers through high school and high school graduates living at home.

In addition to the group sessions, it is sometimes advisable to see individual members on a one-to-one basis on a different schedule or a different day of the week. These sessions should be arranged in those cases where individual problems are complicating the progress expected within family group consultation.

A second method of working consists of seeing an individual family with one or two counselors. This is done when the nature of the problem is such that it cannot be adequately handled in a larger group setting. The usual criteria consists of the intensity of the concern and the immediacy of a crisis situation which may require a crash program to resolve it before a catastrophe ensues. Many of the juvenile court referrals of boys and girls on probation fall within the emergency category. However, after a brief period, in which the intense anxiety is reduced to manageable levels and a crisis is averted, a more comfortable and leisurely schedule becomes possible. Under these conditions, it is advisable to move the family into consultation with a group of families at the earliest opportunity.

One of the prime reasons for placing a single family into a group immediately is that families in trouble are so often isolated from the culture. They have no peer groups of their own. Herein is a primary concern in consultation. Families in trouble have no source of standards, outside of their own individual resources, to use in day-to-day living and experiencing within a complex social order. Learning participation-skills for the social system becomes a primary goal in family consultation. This is best achieved by exposing families to each other under very carefully controlled, learning-environment conditions (Bower, 1965). In this setting, counselors must learn to work as a team so that each can serve as a check and balance against the standards of society, as well as the emergencies of the immediate situation. It calls for innovative and creative know-how on the part of the counselors and becomes a very important learning environment for counselor education.

In summary, family consultation emerged in response to a need for helping youngsters referred from school classrooms to a medical school outpatient clinic. The Outpatient Clinic is the end-of-the-line of social agencies to which the school turns for referral assistance. The new departure in treatment was created because the family participants desired to be seen for a continuing period. The tryout in schools came with counselor enrollees in an N.D.E.A. Counseling Institute. The results combined to motivate the continuation of development work. Further development and study encouraged the formalizing of a method for treatment and a method for graduate counselor-education. Chapter 5 is a description of the latter.

5

The Counselor
and Counselor Education

The Role of the Counselor

The counselor is an active agent-for-change in the family consultation process. There is no such thing as a *neutral* counselor role in family group consultation or family consultation.

Confrontive, interpretive, reflective, empathic, problem-solving, participant-observer behavior is most characteristic of the counselor in family consultation. These methods are much more closely aligned with master-teacher behavior than with psychotherapist behavior.

Learning to *represent the family's condition* is the primary objective in family group consultation. It is necessary for the counselor to get a look at what is happening in the family before any treatment or counseling plan can be devised.

The counselor must "teach" the family to represent its condition. A *first* step is the selection of the family, and the formulation of the consultation group. If this is to be a *group of families*, each family must go through a similar selection process. If, however, it is to be a group consisting only of *one* family and the *counselors*, selection of the family and the counselors constitutes a first step. A *second* step is to take the history of the family and what brings it to its present condition. The process and the content of the history-taking is important. It sets the tone and the climate for learning so essential in family consultation.

Learning *how to tell the family story* begins with the history taking. Learning how to tell the family story is important to most of what happens in family consultation. The first step is to help the family describe a life event. Start with a specific event in which at least two or more of the family participated directly and listen to each person tell about his experiences in such a way that each other person can check this story, his interpretation and his perceptions, against those of the individual talking about the event. There is a considerable period of time essential to carrying out this phase of learning to tell the family story.

Each individual must learn how to represent *his life events*. Individuals begin by relating what happens to each of them at home. The second step is to relate what happens to each *other* person at home. Each other person can come to learn how he is viewed by other members of the family. Each *other* member of the family can come to know how the individual who is relating the event views each of them.

In family consultation, it is extremely important to learn how to read and interpret the non-verbal behavior and non-contextual behavior exhibited by individual family members. Counselors themselves sometimes exhibit these behavior forms, when they are encountering family consultation for the first time. These kinds of behavior must be evaluated in the context of the family condition, and particularly, under the exigencies of the situation in which it occurs. It is extremely important in family group consultation for counselors to use non-verbal and non-contextual behavior to interpret meanings of what is communicated.

Evaluation in family consultation rests almost entirely with the ability to observe changes in the effects of what is communicated in the way the meanings are responded to in verbal, non-verbal, and non-contextual behavior by each family member. The family reporting system is in terms of: How do you view what is happening now? How do you feel about what has happened to the family? Other similar questions help to reveal the family condition.

Progress in family consultation is usually *not* difficult to see. It is relatively easy to see the nature and extent of specific progress, because everything will be acted upon in the *immediate* here-and-now of the consultation sessions. The presence of the counselors will not deter it. There is very little that a family can hide from itself. The symbols used, the signs given, and the meanings attached thereto, in the behavior complex of a family in family consultation seem to become much too complicated for our language to describe. However, there is at least one major constant in family behavior in family consultation:

A family will attempt to continue to behave in the way it presents itself initially, even though major changes in individual behavior have occurred at home and at school. This is an interesting and even curious phenomenon. It becomes more comprehensible if one looks at what constitutes the stability of individual human behavior. Each of us attempts to maintain a constant role in relation to specific situations and individuals. A family unit seems to be able to do a similar thing in family consultation sessions.

Analysis of the content of the statements made by individual family members and by counselors has been attempted by the use of a paradigm (Fullmer and Bernard, 1964). The paradigm is useful if you relate the concept of process to the learning-how-to-learn mentioned above, and the content dimension, to that of the task before the family, or an individual in the family, during family consultation. The use of the paradigm is helpful for beginners but becomes less useful with the experienced counselor in family consultation. It seems that, in our own practice, we have become proficient enough to make the observations and keep the records as part of the direct experience of the family consultation process. The paradigm's value lies primarily in helping the neophyte in family consultation to get some structure imposed upon the ambiguity of the new idea or experience.

Objective criteria for evaluation have been evolved in a study conducted by Irish at the Portland Counseling Center for Adults, during 1964–65.* Dr. Irish used a Q-sort technique to measure the change in attitude among individuals within families during family group consultation. She found that attitudes definitely do change, and that they can be measured by the use of objective instruments. Additional research is indicated to measure the extent, permanence, and direction of behavior modification as reflected in attitudes and overt behaviors, considering specific situations and specific individuals within families.

Subjective criteria are used throughout the process of family consultation in order to maintain some kind of constant climate for learning. The subjective criteria are similar to those used by a master-teacher to conduct a classroom learning environment. They consist primarily of the counselor using his own feelings as a measure of the stress in a situation in order to judge whether or not there is too much or too little anxiety for efficient and effective learning.

Counselor Learning

The initial family contact brings to the surface one of the immediate concerns of counselors, parents, teachers, youngsters, and school ad-

---

* The results of this study are reported in a doctoral dissertation on file at Oregon State University, Corvallis, Oregon.

ministrators: that of finding a suitable starting point for consultation. A counselor conducting the family consultation sessions is considered to be a specialist in altering the behavior of the other person. We have found that the counselor must be prepared to alter his own behavior as a result of the learning experiences inherent in family consultation. Family consultation, as we have practiced it, *always* has been used in a graduate counselor-education program. An education program should involve modification of behavior on the parts of the counselors, their students, and the persons engaged in counseling.

The first message in family consultation is usually identified as a highly specific concrete target-behavior. One family member has been referred for some reason involving behavior and/or learning with the attending expectation that the counselors will "fix" the individual referred. Altering the behavior of a youngster in specific dimension of concrete target-behavior frequently carries the message to the youngster, "Stop being yourself!" Such a confrontation is destined to produce more heat than light. As would be true for any person entering a new situation, it is necessary for the counselors and the family members to work out a means of evolving a collaborative experience. Persons entering a new situation seek reassurance that there is a guarantee of no risk or minimum risk in this new experience. The central concern of all parties involved in a new situation surrounds the concept of *accountability*. Responsibility for what happens rests primarily with the counselor, but the accountability for what happens is *mutually shared* among all the participants in a group counseling or consultation arrangement.

One way of noting this condition in initial sessions in family consultation is watching for polar opposites. When the message system includes messages that say, "You do nothing," or "You do too much," one can only conclude that the person does not know what the other person actually does.

Length of Treatment Under Family Consultation

If some changes have not occurred in the perception of individual family members by the agreed-upon number of sessions, it is our opinion that additional sessions would not help. However, it is possible to make significant progress in six to eight sessions with some families. There is an additional postulation. After a furlough of some months, families may reenter family group consultation sessions and expect desirable results.

If one will look at the family as a total social system, it is possible to assume that only open-ended groups could be maintained for family participation. *Open-ended groups* mean that a family may enter a group of families in consultation, for brief periods of time, withdraw for a period of time, reenter the group and continue consultation. This family might be the same or a different family depending upon the decision and judgment of the counselors. We have found in practice that reentry of a family into ongoing consultation is a rare event. Therefore, it seems that the natural selection by the family of a choice to enter consultation, to leave consultation, and later reenter consultation, is a self-correcting situation. A closed society of groups may be a desirable phenomenon for individual families. There may be certain families who would prefer to enter consultation with certain other families that would continue with them to termination. In practice, we have found that either method is desirable, providing the families agree and make a contract to engage personally in the activity of family consultation. There do not seem to be any undesirable effects of having a family enter an open-ended group, providing they have been brought to the point where they can handle the anxiety they will feel when shown acceptance by the other members of the group. The family group members sometimes open up the new family much too fast. The family group members may be eager to show acceptance and love, or impress the new family. The counselor must be alert to terminate a session after only a few minutes, if this occurs. He may directly intervene. He should explain what is happening to the total group of families. They should shift their interest and emphasis to one of the other families in the group. Any of these foils or combinations is available to the counselor, and should be used with discretion. In summary, it is possible to work with a family under whatever conditions prevail, providing the counselor is comfortable with the conditions and the arrangements. Individual family members may or may not follow willingly the family decision to enter consultation. We have found that *reluctant participation* is much more desirable than absence. Indeed, one of the members of one of the early families in consultation spent three years resisting the idea of family consultation and has since developed into one of our most proficient student-counselor-consultant assistants.

Peer Groups and Reference Groups for Families

Most families who are in trouble do not have adequate access to other persons particularly in terms of peer group and/or reference group relationships. One of the contributions of family group consultation is to increase the frequency of contact between individual family members *within* a family and *among* families, so they can evolve peer groups inside and outside of their own household.

Parents need peer groups and/or reference groups in order to maintain a balance and reality in their orientation toward what children are doing, what they want to do, and what is desirable in terms of the cultural norms. The source of cultural norms is almost exclusively in the hands of other persons. If parents have no access to other persons, they have no way of evaluating, confirming, or questioning any of the criteria they use in establishing limits for their children's behavior, their own behavior, and their contact with other persons.

Siblings sometimes form important peer groups within families. Very little is known about the impact upon behavior modification in family consultation as a result of identifying and exposing peer groups within the sibling group, or helping to form new peer groups within the siblings of a given family. It is generally agreed by the authorities that the existence of sibling peer groups, established among families in family group consultation, is a desirable thing. It has more desirable effect if one of the youngsters in one of the families had been a social isolate. (An isolate is not part of an active peer group or reference group system, inside or outside, of the consultation sessions.)

The extended family can be both a blessing and a curse. Much depends upon the nature of the impact of persons within the extended family or kinship group. In some instances, families perpetuate self-defeating behavior patterns over long periods of time because they do not have adequate access to other persons. Usually their attempts to establish relationships outside of the kinship group have been blocked by some kind of dependence or active intervention on the part of another parent or grandparent. In family consultation, it is *always* good to have contact at least once or twice with all of the persons who have contact with the individual family participating in consultation. It will help the counselors assess the nature of the relationships established, maintained, and reacted to, by the family under study.

The family is the only group in our culture that does not recruit. Among penal groups, psycho-biological families represent elaborate collective fantasies among peers. The incidence of overt competition for new members does not appear (Lamberti, 1963). The girls identified as "parents" in the fantasy families are more aggressive, antisocial, and campaigners against the staff. The father figure is the more masculine type girl; the mother figure is the more feminine. The girls follow an elaborate social system which functions cooperatively as a bio-social unit to insure survival of each member. Without the psycho-biological family and the cooperative behavior between individual members, physical life is jeopardized, and human life is impossible. The human person becomes socialized within the relationships of parent-child-sibling-family structure. Normal association among the father-brother-sister helps the girl develop appropriate psycho-social attitudes and behaviors toward the male sex. A similar condition prevails for the boy and his mother. Some of the most dramatic analogs of the family as a basic phenomenon come from prison literature. The extreme deprivation of life-support systems in solitary confinement brings to the surface the urge to survive and the method for doing it. Common among corrections personnel is the knowledge that every prisoner has his "survival" group. Fantasied or real, they are separated. Improvising and creating a family from what is at hand calls for exceptional ingenuity, especially in solitary confinement where physical nearness is controlled. One prisoner spent over 40 years in solitary and was able to survive by creating several peer groups and/or "families" from which he could get access to the basic relationships necessary for survival as a human being. He started with birds, a bird family, and later with unseen people who needed his bird-doctor advice (Gaddis, 1955).

The family is the primary or first group. Each normal person expands to membership in many peer or reference groups. By changing our roles, within the family, each of us manages to stay close to a family all of our lives.

The Concept of Counselor Teams

The training of apprentice counselors to conduct consultation with families is a continuing concern. We have mentioned that family consultation is an extremely effective method of teaching counseling skills. It is equally productive in helping to train sub-professionals as counselor aides; i.e., teachers, parents, and mature young people. Considerable success has been achieved in attempting to get families to act as assistant counselors. This is usually left on an informal basis, so that the assisting family does not get overburdened with responsibilities and obligations which they might feel if the structure were formalized in any way. In family consultation, when additional families are brought into the group and family *group* consultation is undertaken, there is a direct relationship between the effects of what happens, and the role of the "other" families as assistant counselors. This is expressed in at least three major ways:

1) Confirmation of individual identity for the group; as individuals concerning an individual representation of a behavior, as a family representation of an event, or as a group of persons
2) Validation of behavior for the same groups and individuals as cited above
3) Testing-behavior is an important artifact of family consultation. Testing-behavior is the kind of event in which a person actually practices a new behavior in the presence of other persons, who can respond by giving feedback concerning the impact of the new behavior. The way the behavior is received by other persons

is important to the individual who is performing the testing-behavior. Such a condition is extremely productive for all participants, and particularly, the individual who is attempting to learn a *new* way of behaving.

How to Start Family Group Consultation

It is usually desirable to meet with individual families before they are put into a group with other families. The recommended procedure is to add one family to each group of families, as opposed to convening a group of two or three separate families, for an initial interview period. In keeping with our tradition of showing respect for the family as a unit, we do not classify families according to problems, and place them together according to likenesses or differences, for the effect of similarity or contrast. Persons interested in working with family consultation would be advised to test, under systematic study conditions and research, the effect of the various ways one might *match families* for group consultation. However, family consultation with single families need not concern itself with this issue. It is possible to start a given family on an individual basis without any fanfare or concern for the matching of problems, or the avoidance of certain likenesses, within or among, the several families and their members. We would mention the fact that in our experience, we find greater variation among the members *within* a family than we find differences *between* family units. This notion is very much parallel with the idea that the range of differences within an individual person, may be greater than the variation among a group of individuals on any one criterion or variable.

Types of Sessions

The main types of sessions include the intake sessions, the treatment sessions with individual families, the treatment sessions in group family consultation, and individual one-to-one counseling sessions as needed.

Counselors have to make a judgment concerning, when and if, a particular combination of sessions is indicated for a family. In order to meet the real needs of a family, the counselor should consider possible schedule conflicts in making these arrangements. For instance, it is not wise to create a financial burden on the family by asking the father to take time off from work in order to come to a session. Instead, it is better to make counselors available for late afternoon, evening, and Saturday sessions to accommodate this economic need of the family. There are a number of people in need of counseling help and family consultation sessions who could profit from such a service if it were provided at time other than conventional Monday through Friday working day hours.

Many families will accommodate our needs to work with the entire family group in meeting the learning needs of a youngster in school, if we can plan our schedule so the father and mother, each of whom may be working, can come to the sessions at a time that does not conflict with their working days. The complications are obvious when the father and mother work different shifts. However, we have solved this problem by meeting on a day when both of them are off. Usually, it is possible for them to get employers to arrange their schedules for this purpose if it is approached in a diplomatic and conscientious way.

In the final analysis, we work with that part of the family available to us. If for any reason, it is impossible for one of the partners in the family to be a participating member, we go ahead with family consultation. We follow the assumption that the persons who are available are the persons around whom we can build some kind of solid foundation. We can help people learn to lead, even though they are in a subordinate or dependent position within the family. We do not always succeed as well as we would hope, and indeed, sometimes we fail. However, the overwhelming majority of our experiences support the notion that working with those available to us is a fact of life and a reality with which much can be done.

Variations of Sessions for Individuals

Various sessions should be arranged for individuals in direct response to needs. There are some real limitations on the counselor in a school setting when he attempts to arrange for the variety of sessions sometimes indicated by the intensity and nature of the individual's concerns. However, we take the position that it is desirable to go as far as possible to meet the treatment needs of the individual in each family in counseling.

Variations of Sessions for Families

The consultation sessions must meet the family's basic needs. The extremely complex conditions surrounding most families, and the counseling and the consultation sessions needed to help them, require flexibility and innovative capabilities.

There are many operational limits surrounding the consultation plan and the school. Therefore, it is not possible to make all of the necessary variations appropriate and available to each family. However, everything possible should be done to meet the needs of a family for a variety of sessions surrounding family consultation; i.e., if they need individual sessions as a family, these should be provided; if the family needs access to other families, then family group consultation sessions should be arranged; and if persons within the families need individual counseling, it should be provided.

Counseling Methods

There is a considerable range of counseling methods available for family consultation. They parallel the counseling and treatment methods available in the helping professions. Because the family adds a dimension to the usual educational environment of the school, it is possible to get an increase in the potential effectiveness and efficiency of the working and helping relationships. As contrasted with a medical setting, there are no drugs administered in the family consultation sessions. If individuals in family consultation are under medical supervision of their family doctor or a psychiatrist who helps the school or counseling center, it is well for the counselors to understand the nature of the effects and possible side-effects of the drug therapy conducted concurrently with family consultation. It has been our practice in recent years to urge reduction of the drug intake of participants in families in consultation in order to assess the amount of behavior modification accomplished through the use of family consultation. However, it should be remembered, this move is always made under the supervision of our consulting psychiatrist. If the school system retains a consulting psychiatrist, this is one of the ways his services can be used.

The methods of treatment and/or counseling currently available in the helping-relationship-professions are as follows: 1) supportive, 2) intervention, 3) coercion, 4) environment manipulation, and 5) permissive.

Systems of treatment and/or counseling available to the helping professions are as follows: 1) intrapsychic, 2) desensitization — sensitization, 3) logical-intellectual-reason, and 4) drug therapies, etc.

The methods and systems of counseling utilized by the helping professions contain certain behaviors *prescribed* for the counselor or psychotherapist. Among these are the following: 1) active-passive roles for the counselor, 2) observation, the neutral-observer, 3) observation-critical, the benevolent authoritarian or father-figure, 4) the participant-observer or anthropological data gatherer, 5) reflecting or non-directive, client-centered Rogerian type, 6) interpreting, judging, and valuing master-teacher 7) confronting or representative-of-the-society type, 8) empathic type who communicates understanding and love as a supportive measure, 9) problem-solving type (including many of the behaviorists and operant conditioning devotees), and 10) strong leader or politician environment-manipulator, social engineer type.

All of these are possible types of behavior practiced by the counselor-psychotherapist in the helping relationship.

In family consultation we rarely find ourselves in a position of direct power over the family or any of its individual members. The counselor certainly does have access to many of the avenues to power within the family, consisting of 1) *interrupting* the family and having it meet with him in family consultation sessions, and 2) *intervening* in the family affairs by sharing with them as they relate their experiences during a family event, and 3) *influencing*, exerted by the counselor as he responds to what he hears and to what he participates in with the family. In family group consultation sessions, all of these influences are multiplied by the numbers and types of persons, and the reactions they have to similar circumstances, as the family shares its individual reactions to its own family events. In family consultation, it is safe to assume that almost any one of the possible counseling treatment methods would be appropriate. However, it is always a counselor's judgment to determine what combination of counseling methods, systems of counseling, and counseling behavior will be employed. This should not exclude drug therapies and supervision by an M.D., a psychiatrist consulting with the family consultation group. The only limits for possible application of different helping relationships methods would rest with the competency and training of the counselors conducting the consultation sessions.

Personal Contracts and Family Consultation

Family consultation, to be effective, must have some kind of informal or formal agreement procedure. We have found the *personal contract* a very useful device in effecting these agreements. A family is a complex unit, with certain sanctions surrounding it. These must be respected. In order to avoid invasion of privacy, to avoid disrupting the family operational unit, and to keep from creating unrealistic expectations on the part of individual members of the family, it is necessary, and desirable, to have some kind of agreement concerning the expectations, the goals, and the methods of consultation, including the length of time and the number of sessions.

The usual method is to see the family initially for a session without making any formal agreement beyond the intake appointment. Following some assessment during the initial session, it is desirable to spend some time with the family deciding whether or not the family wants to proceed with family consultation. If the family desires *not* to come back, the "contract" can be terminated. If the family wishes to go on, there should be some exploration of their reaction to the fact that during the first two or three sessions a family usually experiences what we have come to call "the blush of health." This is a period during which most of the family members *try* to effect some kind of modification of their own behavior. It usually takes the form of withholding certain behaviors which knowingly cause stress for other members of the family. The result is a kind of "instant cure." We have followed the principle that if a family knows what is apt to happen to it, the effects of shock and other anxiety-producing reactions can be significantly reduced, if not fully nullified. We attempt to help the family see its future in terms of a number of sessions, from six to twelve. A minimum of six is felt to be necessary to effect any change at all; and a maximum of twelve is necessary to prevent the family consultation sessions from becoming part of the family's problem. A furlough, and perhaps reentry into the family consultation relationship, might be indicated but this can be reviewed in the negotiations for an additional contract.

Taboos and Family Consultation

Taboos are a part of our cultural heritage. There are some things one may not do. These are known to almost every one who grows up in our American culture. Therefore, simply *do not do those things the society frowns upon,* and the rule will usually carry you through the family consultation sessions. For example, one of these taboos concerns the status of the father and the mother as parents within the family; one does not attempt to replace, nullify, or discredit parents. The weakest of fathers must be supported and confirmed, in the eyes of the family, as a valuable and contributing member. This can be done without, in any way, relating the negative loading of some of the practices, dependencies, or needs of such a person. A second rule that we have found useful is to respect the family as a unit by always asking its permission before attempting any action that would reflect upon the family in terms of any of the societal taboos. If the family gives permission, it is tantamount to being invited into their home, in which case one behaves as a guest of the house, not as an autocrat, or authority figure, and certainly not by taking over the reins of the family unit, and running it. In summary, we would say that one should always defer to the family unit, and any of its traditional structures, including the role of the father and the role of the mother, as persons above and beyond whom there is no authority over the family.

Myths and the Presenting-Problem

The myth that is most commonly encountered in all family consultation, is the one that says, "fix the presenting problem." It is almost never possible to *fix* the presenting problem. It is possible to change the behavior and reactions to behavior within the family to the point where the presenting behavior is no longer anxiety-producing and therefore is no longer a problem to the family.

There are two other major issues related to the myth of fixing the presenting-problem. First is the proposition of symptom reduction. The second is the counter-proposition that education, counseling, and any treatment method avoid taking on the direct responsibility of changing a specific behavior.

Symptom reduction is sometimes absolutely essential before any other concerns can be attended by the family. The behavior of the child may be so disruptive and so extreme that, until it has been modified, the family cannot effectively bring its forces and resources to bear upon any other concern. In behavior, there is an added factor that if a person is to stop doing one thing and start doing a second thing, he no longer has *time* to do the first thing. This represents a kind of *substitute behavior* that eliminates one kind of behavior by substituting another kind. Symptom reduction is looked upon in various ways by practicing counselors, but, in family consultation, it is a highly effective and useful means of meeting the myth of fixing the presenting problem.

The avoidance of responsibility-taking by the counselors is no doubt the simplest means of managing the myth referred to above. It is by no means the most productive way of handling this kind of condition. It is much more advisable to go ahead and assume the responsibility for fixing the presenting problem, even though it is considered a myth. Myths may be quite useful if they can be turned toward a goal that is desirable in meeting the expectations of those persons engaged in family consultation. The decision involves a large measure of judgment on the part of the counselor, and must be assumed as one of the responsibilities attending the work in family consultation.

Counselor-Education Function

The conditions for learning include the necessity for creating some stress. Stress results from meeting ambiguous situations and facing the necessity of imposing some structure upon the ambiguity of the life condition in order to differentiate oneself from the environment. In family consultation, the setting is naturally stress-producing for all members of the family and for the counselors. This is one of the elements that adds to the power of family consultation as a counselor-education method. In order to benefit from learning opportunities in family consultation, a counselor and a family member must *practice new behavior*. The family consultation setting allows for psychological safety of the individual practicing new behavior, while simultaneously providing a direct experience for all participant-observers in the process.

Each person learns how to determine, or "know," where he is within the interaction. To characterize this, we have used such terms as being "tuned-in," or "turned on," and "getting the signals." The exercise involves something we have come to call the *process of participants earning their listening.* The idea is that, in order to be heard ourselves, we must first earn our listening from the other person, by having ourselves tuned-in to what he is saying. This is the message system that is automatically characterized by concern, acceptance, and mutual regard or mutuality. It is necessary for the counselor to know where he is within the interaction in order for him to make the new kind of contribution; that is, in order to disseminate information about any new activity that will affect the lives of each individual family member. This requires a new kind of competence. The competence is a how-to-disseminate information about any new activity. The student counselor will need to earn his status with the family members. Prestige will not be thrust upon him.

Implementation

It is usually necessary to have a fairly well defined set of implementation procedures (mechanisms) for getting conditions arranged so that new information can be disseminated. The central concern of the implementation procedures used by the counselor or the consultant is "how to make clear" the information or contribution about any new activity.

There are certain kinds of conditions in which a news-item type dispatch, a factual statement concerning the information to be disseminated, best serves the purpose. The counselor or consultant can then invite a response regarding how the members of the family see the information, the new activity, or the new competence to be learned. The power of this procedure lies in its ability to avoid the tender trap of making suggestions to the family. The reason for trying to avoid the trap of making suggestions derives from the assumption that whatever way the family is presently using — that is, the old way of doing a thing — must have substance or reason behind it and foundation under it. Any habitual or ritualistic way of doing something includes some assumed efficiency that might be lost if a suggestion were made, out of context, by the counselor.

One assumption the counselor can make concerning any new competence to be developed is that it will be a difficult task because *all new learning* will cause some rearrangement or readjustment of the old patterns of doing things within the family. At this point an analogy may be helpful to clarify the reasons for considering these conditions for change so important in the direct experience of family and family membership. If one imagines a network of highways or roads interconnecting or leading from place "A" to place "B" to place "C," and he wishes to change them, he is faced with the choice of whether to redesign the entire pattern of highways or access routes or whether to look at the map or pattern of highways as they are laid out and note where shortcuts or improvements could be made in the existing system. Obviously, we would not want to limit the family consultation process so that we would assume one might do any one of these things under given conditions. But, for the moment, consider the advisability of just building a road without knowing where it begins or will end. Such procedure is comparable to making a suggestion to a family when one is not a member of that family.

In an attempt to summarize the basic concepts involved, and how one develops a new kind of competence within a family in family consultation, let us say simply that it is fun to be in on new learning. If we can get a contract with a family to share this concern or assumption, it is easier to move into the possibility of modification of present behavior patterns or even to introduce some new competencies on the part of one of the members of the family. Charging ahead with only one member of the family is destined to be viewed as a kind of provocation by all other members of the family. It is wiser to work toward pooling the resources of the parents, the youngsters, teachers, administrators, and other counselors. Each family is connected to an interlocking system of significant other persons in any life situation. It is necessary to have access to as many of these individuals as possible in order to determine some way of proceeding, and to get a look at the pattern of the old way of doing things in this family. In order to add the situational dimension, it is necessary to do this with the family *as a unit* at one time. In family consultation, we focus upon the learning environment created by the family, in which each individual participates. In this context, "individual" refers to significant other persons as well as members of the immediate family group. In some'socioeconomic classes in American society, this will include the relationship or kinship pattern of the extended family. A central question always in the minds of the counselors is, "What can we do to help the youth learn and who must be involved to accomplish this end?"

The central question of what we can do to help shifts the emphasis from a person-centered orientation to a problem-centered orientation.

Problem orientations make the conditions for learning situationally determined. Problem-centered orientations and situationally-determined learning environments make allowance for inclusion of contributions by each individual affected by the decisions made, the behaviors modified, and the actions to be taken within a family. Each parent describes experiences with the different members of the family, and each youngster describes experiences with the different members of the family. In doing this, it is possible to get active participation by all parties interested in the family condition. The arrangements required for working in family consultation parallel the kinds of arrangements promoted by helping agencies in the mental health programs for the poor. Poverty programs carry the stipulation that those persons affected by actions taken must be included in the planning. Mental health is the result of active participation in the decision making concerning basic problems shared by all members in a given group. The validity of this assumption is supported by the experiences we have had in family consultation.

In family consultation settings, it is immediately apparent that all people do not respond to the same treatment. Each individual will have unique response patterns to the same counseling process. This may be the same potential that gives each individual human being a kind of infinite variation index. Almost always, it has been our experience that an individual's *specific* behavior is not a highly predictable phenomenon. However, general patterns of behavior within a given cultural group, within a given sub-culture or class of society, tend to be relatively stabilized and predictable.

Family consultation requires that close scrutiny be given to discovering what it is that a family has handled successfully in previous times. It seems reasonable to assume that many things have been handled successfully in previous situations, and it is important for the counselor to remember to reward such previous successes. Following recognition of the adequacy of certain behavior in certain areas of concern, the counselor can begin to talk about new ways of handling the situation or situations included in the presenting problem. It is important to talk about new approaches, try them out, and then evaluate the results of the trial period. Once this has been completed, the counselors may negotiate with the family on the basis of new compromises with existing practices and patterns of behavior. This becomes a continuing search for alternative ways of behaving in situations which have produced problems in the past.

Target areas for behavior modification should be identified. The work should be in connection with some phase of developing alternatives that result in modifying the behavior applicable to these target areas. The target areas are *always* problem-centered areas of concern.

Target problems may be identified and specified following the selection of those areas causing the most concern at the moment the counselor meets with the family. The advantage of identifying *specific problems* lies in providing a basis for arranging a priority system so that each problem may be attacked in a sequence leading from the here-and-now point toward a goal that has been confirmed as important to the family and/or to individual members of the family.

The counselor consultant should plan with the family and with the individual members of the family. The purpose is to establish some kind of working contract between counselor and family. The plan should be carefully specified in terms of what is *possible*. On whom does the plan rely for its realization? The placing of responsibility is important. Allowance for inclusion of a number of reasonable alternatives within the plan is of equal importance. The plan should run for a reasonable length of time and be capable of termination. Open-ended plans with no closure in view tend to overload a family which is in trouble. Families in trouble need the reinforcement of achieving short-term goals. These achievements can be used as positive evidence to support feelings of adequacy as human beings and as a family unit. It has been our experience that ten or twelve sessions, running on a one-session-per-week basis, constitute the upper limits of productive time in family group consultation. There is some evidence that six to eight sessions represent the usual amount of time necessary to achieve some results with a family. Many families will need no more than six or eight sessions, and some families will need more than twelve sessions. However, it is recommended that not more than twelve sessions be contracted for at any one time. We have used the concept of a *furlough* for the family between an agreed-upon sequence of sessions. Each group of sessions may range from eight to twelve in a sequence. We think that counselors working with family consultation should try for five to ten sessions as their usual period for working with a family or a group of families in a school setting.

Individual Families in Counseling

Most of the literature on family counseling reflects the pattern of working with one family at a time. Family consultation experience shows that some families should receive help in private and under such intense conditions that it is advisable to see the single family on an individual basis. Persons may also be seen individually. This should not be confused with seeing an individual family, i.e., one family group with the counselors at one session. Family consultation does not necessarily restrict work to individual families. It is possible to see families separately and concurrently see them in a group of other families, as well as seeing individual persons from within a family on a one-to-one basis. It is not necessary for the same counselor to do all of the work with a given family unit and/or individuals. The advantages of having more than one counselor working with the same family are somewhat self-evident. As team members in a co-counseling situation, more than one counselor is concerned at the same time with various aspects of a given family and its problems. The cooperative arrangement can add considerable strength to the impact achieved in the family consultation process.

The team counseling approach of family consultation greatly enhances the counselor-education dimension. The neophyte counselor, as a graduate student enrolled in counselor education, is much better situated to have opportunities for learning if he can share in the team approach to family consultation.

The Counselor Group as a Model for Learning

Family consultation is conducted by a team of counselors. Counselor education is provided by the group of persons engaged in: 1) counseling the family or families; 2) the team members — usually two counselors; 3) three to five observers who participate when the situation makes it seem appropriate; and 4) the supervisor(s) or counselor-educator(s).

Item 3 above refers to the persons who "sit in" to learn enough to launch their own groups. The laboratory model is a supervised experience for each participant, including the family members. The "group" is the crux of the learning-how-to-learn model for counselor education. Each member of the training group of counselors and supervisor(s) becomes engaged in giving and receiving feedback from each other member. *No one is immune to the critical evaluation given by each member to each other member.* Everyone is on an "equals" basis to help create a learning environment, where supervisor, leader, and observer merge in the teaching-learning process. The creation of the learning environment is the unique contribution family consultation provides for counselor education.

Some criteria used to evaluate the progress of each participant have been identified. When a person (counselor, parent, observer, or "other") begins to remark, "I'm in the group" . . . "We constitute a group" . . . "I want to join this group," etc., we have noticed the start of behavior change in that person. Lewin and Grabbe (1945) maintain that behavior does not change until the person changes values. To change values, one must become a member of a new group. The magnitude of changing behavior is equated with changing cultures by an individual. The establishing of such a nuclear group by the counselor educator is a prerequisite to creating a viable family consultation program.

The treatment power of family consultation is probably no greater than any of the established methods and systems of counseling. The counselor education method provided by family consultation has continued to encourage our practice because of the learning outcomes for counselors. Hopefully, we will have encouraged others to try their own versions of family consultation. Dialogue is an important next step.

6

Sequential Development
of Family Consultation

The movement of a family into consultation takes on the procedural variations familiar to almost any educational endeavor, such as beginning school, going to the family doctor, arranging to attend church school, or deciding to go to a PTA meeting. Briefly, the family must decide, for some reason or set of reasons, that it wishes to participate in family consultation. The reason a family comes to family consultation is a highly personal matter. The decision, once it has been made, usually contains several common elements:

1) The family has decided that, in the interest of one of its members, all of the family is required to participate in family consultation.

2) The family wants to do what is best for its total membership. The need is apparent in the case of one of its members who appears to be in trouble. There is a demand for action.

3) The crisis is a personal matter and may not be apparent to external view by other persons outside the family.

4) The problem may be obscured to the family itself and be apparent only to outsiders such as teachers, school administrators, counselors, ministers, or the juvenile court.

5) A family may come because its members have heard it is a good thing. They do not want to miss any opportunities for their youngsters

to learn. They are interested in learning, as parents, so they wish to become part of an educational program designed to help parents and the school improve the educational experiences of youngsters.

Interaction is a primary message system (Hall, 1959), and consists of any form of communicating, one person to another. Messages are exchanged as a mother communicates at many levels with her child. She may use speech or non-verbal and non-contextual behavior. Any of the several ways, including touching and cuddling, are usual ways a mother communicates acceptance, love, security, and many other meanings. Speech is the most common interaction among human beings. Speech is not necessarily the only carrier of messages received by the "other" person. Speech, in its pure form, operates usually on what we would call a *cognitive interchange*. This is an instance where factual information is exchanged for its own sake. Any interpretation of meaning communicated by inflection of voice, the articulation and context of metaphors takes us immediately into a different level of communication and a different set of messages with highly personal meanings (Finder, 1966). All personal meanings are connected to the message system — *touching*. Language is seen as a form of symbolic touching.

In family consultation we are concerned with the interaction among and between people on the following several levels: 1) mothering, 2) cognitive interchange, 3) information exchange, 4) validation of behavior, 5) affective behavior (feelings transmitted), 6) confirmation behavior, and 7) confirmation of a way of valuing (thinking).

The counselor consultant watches for the meanings that are being exchanged among the family members: 1) from the family as a group to each of its members, 2) from one person to another within a family, 3) from the family personality to the "outside." This central concern continues during the entire period of consultation. It is the central concern in each exchange and each interaction that takes place.

All information is gathered and interpreted within a frame of reference tempered by the interaction patterns and the exchange of meanings concept. Each counselor will attempt to explain the meanings of the various kinds of behavior encountered in family consultation. The counselor's behavior becomes a part of what must be explained. This process is a continuing concern in family consultation.

Interview Sessions in Family Consultation: Delineation of Aspects

Intake Interview: Session One

1. The information gathering process begins at the intake interview, including any previous communications with the family. Factual content is incidental to the central concern of the messages that are ex-

changed among the members of a family preceding, during, and following a reported event. The *central* concern is: What message is being sent? What message is being received? Are they the same? Do they represent a shared consensus of feeling, emotion, and cognitive content? What conflicts exist? Are the conflicts enabling? Are the conflicts disabling? The questions asked above are usually not answered in the first intake session. Indeed, sometimes, we have never achieved a satisfactory answer to some of these questions. However, we take note of all information that is given, the context in which it is shared, the method and protocol by which it is given, and the restrictions, including the omissions and denials, that surround what is shared through the interaction process during the intake interview.

2. An explanation of family group consultation process is included as part of the intake interview. The counselor must explain to the family what is expected, what family consultation can do, what its limits appear to be, and what a family must commit itself to in order to participate in the process of family consultation. The families are told they will meet together for as many as twelve sessions for the purpose of consulting with two or more professional counselors and each other person in the group. They are told that up to fifteen persons may convene together. As many as three families may join a group, and meet together each week for 1½ to 2 hours.* All of these things are important because, without them, the family can make no clear-cut commitment to continue for enough sessions to allow the process to have some impact upon the operational functions within the family.

3. There is a preparation for involvement that must take place during the initial sessions with a family. Among these are the necessary steps in learning to relate to "outsiders" the significant events that take place in the life space of each individual within the family. This is much more difficult than would appear on the surface. The reason for much of this concern has come from our experience with attempting to interpret what is said about a given event in the life of a youngster within a family as compared to our own experience. Very often our own experience does not qualify within the system used by a given family. Therefore, we must learn to understand what has happened within that family, and the context within which it happened. In order to comprehend the meaning to an individual within the family, it is necessary to get some *common experience with the family*. This is

---

* The first half of the consultation session is spent with *every* family member (in each family) present. The second half of the consultation session is spent with the parents in one section and the children in a second section. Each meeting is led by one of the two (team) counselors. Additional counselors may be present. They should be there regularly as part of the group(s). The shared leadership of a group by more than one counselor is the significant variable in the training model for family consultation. Each person present should participate.

what we mean by preparation for involvement. The counselors must prepare to become involved with the family. The family must prepare to involve itself with the counselor(s) over a long enough period of time for them to share common experiences.

The counselors prepare the family for the kind of openness to experience that will be expected of each family member as consultation progresses. They are reminded that each person is provided "equal time" or the opportunity to relate to any other member of the family. The interpersonal contract must insure *complete* safety for everyone. No retaliation (punishment) will result from "my" openness, "my" behavior within the consultation sessions.

Each other person, in turn, is permitted to feed back to appropriate persons any feelings, thought, or concerns he has a desire to share. In this way, each family member learns carefully to examine specific details in a given problem situation. The counselor's task is to keep the situation safe enough to be candid.

As events are described, the family will learn to become aware of how interpersonal relationships create conditions of healthy or malignant conflict. The arrangement for more than one family to meet together at the same time provides the arena (climate) for creating the opportunities essential to encounter the kind of learning described above.

4. Description of the physical setting is essential because it is at variance with much of the helping profession protocol. In the first place, the family is not seen in exclusively private and protected conditions. The family is seen in a semi-public arrangement, as a result of having other families and counselors present in the consultation situation. Their presence assists in getting some kind of validation check on the perceptions of each counselor. We have maintained a training setting so that other persons can learn from watching the procedure of family consultation and discover what it consists of and how to conduct it. With training and involvement as the key concepts, the family consultation setting is physically different from the usual arrangement of family physician, with his private cubicle or counseling cubicle.

No one person can establish himself as the fountainhead of all wisdom. It is out of the dialogue within the group that new levels of understanding conventional cultural wisdom emerge. To begin such a process, the family is asked to respond to questions: "What issues are you facing as a family?" We ask each person in turn: "How do you see yourself in the family? What is your role? How important are you to the family? Do you make a difference?"

The intake interview is a time for gathering information, of making an explanation to the family concerning the process of family consultation, to prepare for involvement of the counselor(s) with the family over a period of time. It is a time to describe physical setting so that its arrangement is a safe and pleasant place for the family to convene.

Recording information for the folder is restricted to what the counselors can recall as significant highlights from the information gathered. (Do not take notes! Tape recording is permitted.)

In addition to the interview itself, there is the necessary identification information taken on a form or schedule that includes names, dates, address, phone numbers, family doctor-name and number, the family names of all the members, birth dates, and all of the other significant vital statistics necessary to identify a family.

No summary of a session should be more than one-half page typewritten and it should be very carefully worded so that it will not become a problem to anyone in the family or to the counselor for having included his speculations with his observed facts. Factual information that is part of the public record is admissible. Opinions, speculations, hopes, aspirations, and wishes of the counselor or of individual members of the family should be excluded from the record. Anything significant can be remembered. This is the principle under which we function. What is forgotten probably doesn't matter because it will not be available to immediate application anyway (conscious recall).

Take careful notes about the interpersonal *touching behavior* in a family. The symbolic and physical contact, one person to another, is a message system the counselors can begin using immediately at intake.

Session Two

During session two, we are concerned with information gathering. We do not make this a primary concern in any sessions beyond session one and the intake interview. However, information gathering is a part of every contact with a family, whether by phone or in person, and in whatever session pertinent information is shared. There are several items regarding family relationships which the counselors should be particularly careful to observe. Unless the following are critically examined, it is all too easy to be misled by the folklore which is characteristically transmitted — and folklore will be presented as family members attempt the face-saving that is a necessary part of family identity and integrity.

1. It is very important to take note of the members of the nuclear family who are present at session one. Very often, the person who needs the most help will be absent in this first session. This absence is so significant that it should not be rationalized by the counselor(s). The alibi that will be given by the significant other person in the family may be the most significant initial clue shared. Take careful note of the name of the person and the family role of that person e.g., mother, or

father, or sister, or brother. Who makes the explanation for the absent member? The only exception to this rule would be if the counselor were not careful in scheduling the session when all members of the family *could* be present.

2. The counselors should take note of the relationships that exist between and among the members of the family. This is an ongoing and extremely important aspect of the first session. Counselors should note the peer groups among siblings and how these are used. Take careful note of whether the parents have a peer group(s).

3. Take note of the control factors in the family. Who has the power to control this family? How is the power of control of the family members executed? What is the impact of the way the family is controlled on each individual member of the family?

4. Note the involvement of each member in the family consultation session. The degree of involvement of an individual within the family is extremely important to subsequent information gathering concerning the meanings that are exchanged among the members. A person who has a limited involvement in the family consultation session one will often have an extremely important impact upon the family as a whole.

5. Take note of the kind of involvement in which each individual member participates. The family consists of a number of kinds of involvement including verbal, non-verbal and non-contextual behavior. The message system of a family usually reflects the kind of involvement maintained by each individual member.

6. The session may start off by the counselor's question: "Well, how has it been going?" A brief introjected remark or question is designed to start whatever the family wishes to discuss. The counselors should not choose the subject. Usually, the family will respond initially by some superficial remark. Leading on from the remark a counselor asks, "How did it go?" or "What happened?" The counselors try to get the individual family members to describe an event. Each person gives his version of the same event.

> As he listens, the counselor makes careful note of the following factors in an event: (1) time, (2) place, (3) significant persons taking part in the event, and (4) the reporting individual's perception of what happened. It should be noted that he keeps track of *each participant's* account of an event. He checks the description of the event over and over as each person describes it. Out of these data, clear patterns begin to emerge. (Fullmer and Bernard, 1964)

The counselors begin to get a notion of what the loyalties are, the alliances, and the contracts which may exist in the family. He uses these notions to check out with the members what they really are. In a family, for example, where the mother appeared to try to meet her son on his terms in exchange for his loyalty, it seemed pertinent for the counselor to reflect that she might have disqualified herself as mother when she attempted this bargain. The likely pain and anxiety engendered by such a reflection may result in some such client rejoinder as, "What would you do?" or "Tell me what I should do," to which the counselor avoids responding directly. In an effort to keep the responsibility where he believes it belongs, with the owner of the behavior, he would respond by saying something like, "Let's talk about the alternatives available to you. What do you think you could do? How do you think a mother should act?" Should the person be unable to respond, the questions are directed to the group. (Irish, 1966)

Session Three

1. In session three, direction is given by the counselors to the family. The leadership of the counselors cannot be subordinated to a permissive stance because there is not enough clarification at this point for the family to initiate its own action. If the controlling member of the family is particularly ascending, leadership may be deferred to some later session before the counselors can give direction to the work in family consultation. The guiding principle here is simply that in family consultation we assume that, if direction could come from within the family, it would have been operating and family consultation would not have become necessary. Therefore, the counselors take responsibility and are accountable for the direction of movement which will be pursued during the consultation.

2. Session three is the continuing of the systematic description of events including time, place, significant other persons, and the reporting individual's perception of what happened. What happened to me? What happened to each other person?

The interpretation of the impact upon other individuals concerning the behavior within the description given of an event by a certain individual will remain in the realm of speculation on the part of the counselors. However, the same process will be engaged in by each other member of the family.

Until now, the counselors have accepted reporting of events in terms of other persons. Now group members are asked to use first person singular, "I," in place of "he" or "she" or "they," as an event is reported. The focus is directed toward the personal meaning for the person telling the story. The individual is encouraged to own (hold title to) his perception of what happened in the event as he reports it. The same event, reported by each other family member, gives the counselors the data necessary to hypothesize the pattern of behavior in a family, to see how it goes with each person. Each individual is encouraged to begin evaluations of his own behavior. He may say, "I didn't realize I felt that way," or "that's new to me."

3. During session three, it is good to identify what loyalties and alliances exist within the families and among which members. It is important to note the personal contracts that exist within a family. It will give some indication concerning whether contracts can be made with the counselors to carry on family consultation. In the first three meetings, including the intake interview, session one, and session two in most cases, it is not yet established that a family will continue in family consultation. The crucial meetings are sessions four and five. During sessions four and five, decisions are usually made by the family to continue or to terminate family consultation. If the decision is to terminate, sessions four and five do not occur.

> It is intended that by the third session individuals become aware that other families have problems and discussion seems to become more open. A remark such as, "My daughter is that way, too, but I'm not worried about it," may be accepted as supportive. As confidence is gained, individual group members become less the outsiders and more the helping persons. Suggestions or solutions are proffered by members of the group. (Irish, 1966)

By the end of session three, the counselors have spent enough time with the family to establish some measure of involvement with them. The common experiences shared in approximately six hours of direct contact with the family is sufficient to establish some interpersonal interaction contracts.*

Session Four

1. During session four, it is important to gain further practice in the reporting of events within the life space of the family. Each individual must relate his experiences within the same shared experience or event of the family. It is through the similarities and discrepancies as reported by individuals concerning the *same event* within a family that counselors begin to see the intricacies of relationships within the interaction pattern of a family. The meanings that are exchanged between the members during the relating of these events further expands the notation on the loyalties, alliances, contracts, and other existing relationship patterns within a family.

2. The individuals within a family will begin to evaluate their own behavior. Each will do so in terms of what he hears himself say and

---

* A contract is an agreement with another person or group that prescribes limits, obligations, expectations, and conditions regarding mutual actions for specific purposes.

how he interprets the feedback he gets from other members in the group. The counselor may or may not have achieved enough status within the family interaction to be received as a contributing member on the evaluation dimension. However, it is usually true that a father or a mother will depend heavily upon the counselor to sustain a position of adequacy within the family structure. It is very important that the family not have the father or other significant person, including mother, or sister, or aunt, discredited by the behavior of the counselor. The family consultation will serve no useful purpose in the continuing family concern or plan if it is not designed to clarify a productive role (position) for each member.

The principle we operate under is as follows: Do not take away anything from the family which you as a counselor(s) are not prepared to replace *in person* over the continuing period of the future. This principle is so pervasive that it seems to us impossible to underestimate its importance to the family. It restricts the counselor(s) and also offers a guideline for participation within family group consultation.

3. The consultative process is engaged in by other families' members as well as *within* the family's membership.

. . . the most obvious demonstration of commitment is the attendance at the sessions of the individual members. However, other forces may be at work which result in attendance of some members. For example, coercion may be used by parents to get youngsters to attend or a reluctant spouse may be pressured into presenting himself to and in the group. If such possibilities suggest themselves to the counselors, they should check them out by confronting the person with his seeming behavior. A question may be put, such as, "Why do you come here?" or "For whom do you come here?"

In addition to gauging the commitment of the members of the group by their presence, there is another way. Since the first session, the counselors have been asking the individual in the group to describe events and problem situations as they happened. By the fourth session, the counselors have had some direct experience of events as they happen in the group. . . . The counselors ask themselves how well the descriptions offered by the individuals conform to what they, the counselors, observe happening. . . . The counselor reflects what he sees, consistency or discrepancy, and asks the person to react to his reflection. . . . He (the individual) is encouraged to focus on himself in relation to his problems. His willingness to do this may be a gauge of his commitment. (Irish, 1966)

4. It is important during session four to take careful note of the commitment of the family to family consultation. This is assessed by

looking at the attendance pattern and the degree of direct participation by membership within the family (those present) in consultation.

Session Five

Session five is the beginning of the continuing commitment to family consultation. At this point, the counselors and the family(s) have had enough involvement to establish some common ground of communication of messages and meanings individual-to-individual.

1. The direct experience of the counselor in the events as they have happened in group consultation is available for comparison with the accounts given by members of the family of the life events that have been happening outside family group consultation sessions. In brief, the counselor(s) now has enough direct experience with the family to compare the counselor assessment of what happens with what is reported by a given member of the family.

2. The family group may be asked if they discuss the events that occur in family consultation outside of the family consultation session on their own time. This will give an idea concerning the commitment and involvement of the family as a group and of the members within the family as individual participants.

3. Session five is the time to bring the individual membership of the family into the mainstream of the ongoing dynamics of family behavior. Individual behavior of a family member may not yet be sufficiently differentiated from group behavior or group identity within a family to be isolated and discussed separately. However, it is important to note the *adherence* to the topic under discussion or the amount of *digression* or *drifting* from the point of concern. It should be remembered that in family consultation, as in individual counseling, there is a tendency to avoid discussion of items that are embarrassing, crucial, or culpable. Is the person wandering away toward a safe topic or safe areas of concern?

Lack of commitment to consultation from each member may be characterized by a tendency of the group "to wander" through the session, never focusing for long on any issue. . . . Some statement such as, "We don't seem to be able to stay with one subject very long today. I wonder what is going on?" . . . If the counselors feel there is a serious lack of commitment demonstrated, this should be made known to the group since it is felt that movement is questionable under these circumstances.

. . . By the time of the fifth session some members of the group will be observed using the counseling skills they have learned. They will be heard to ask others . . . "I don't think I understand what you are saying. What I thought you said was . . . Can you straighten me out?" (Irish, 1966)

4. Counselors engaged in family consultation will occasionally encounter individual members of a family who appear very intense concerning the specific problem a family presents while actually shielding the possibility of exploring other potential problem areas within the family domain. This is a kind of offense that is used by the family to defend against in-depth exploration of additional family concerns.

5. By the close of session five, ample time has elapsed to prepare a family for some real decision-making concerning its commitment to the ongoing process of family consultation. Whether the family will expose itself to its own behavior, or whether it will continue to play games with the counselors, should be completely clarified by the beginning of session six.

A Principle: Each family will struggle to present the facade they perceive the culture expects even when the act of struggling is self-defeating.

Session Six

1. In session six, there is more display of skills learned by the family members in the process of family consultation. Family group members may exchange these skills and help to teach each other the method of reporting, the method of giving feedback, and the process of analyzing the potential interpretations resident in the skills and knowledge of group members. There is a considerable amount of direct interaction at the level achieved in session six. Unless this is true, something has been hindering the systematic development of the process of family consultation. Counselors should be good trouble-shooters and eliminate roadblocks to good family interaction among its members. Unless this has happened, nothing really has changed in the life space of the family. The counselor's one major contribution is to provide a place where the family members can *all* join in the interaction — can talk to each other and be heard or listened to.

2. The level of maturity in most family consultation experiences is greatly changed by the time session six is reached. Individual group members will ask other group members to look at *his* (my) behavior. The person is asking for both confirmation and validation of his behavior and, consequently, himself. Most significant to the learning condition, he is establishing a *style* by which he can get feedback from other persons in forms useful to him so that modification or change may become a conscious choice condition rather than a controlled consequence.

They will be asking one another to look at his own behavior, pointing out the difference between saying, "You upset me," and saying, "I'm feeling upset, and it seems to be related to you. I wonder what is bothering me." He is being asked to look at his own behavior instead of focusing on the behavior of another in the situation.

. . . Specific incidents, occurring in the group, are used to confront a person with what he does, and what it seems to do to others. . . . The individuals are encouraged to consider changes which they can implement in their own families while comparing such possible solutions to those used in the other families. . . . The sessions beyond the fifth, whether the goal (or contract) is eight sessions or twelve, are used similarly. (Irish, 1966)

Each individual member must learn how to present feedback to the person who is asking, in a way that will not destroy the person or the group. This is significant learning in an interdependent society. Without it, no one can criticize anyone because of the tender mercies that must be shown in such a social situation. Tender loving care (TLC) is a guideline for all feedback systems and all content. Without this precaution, the individual who opens himself to evaluation by other persons is exposing himself, making himself vulnerable, in ways that he cannot defend against. These conditions should not be in any way confused with pity or sympathy, which are condescending messages in behavior.

3. The group members, by session six, will have learned to relate to each other as equals. The station in life or the corporate structure of the culture is the usual guide to the person-to-person interaction process so necessary in the normal ongoing contract-making of interpersonal relationships.

Equals are never condescending nor patronizing. Equals can be open and direct in their interaction. Equals may cut off communication with one another, but the "other" one may feel free to react to being cut off. The hallmark of communication among equals is the openness or realness we attempt to achieve in family consultation. Each person is encouraged to stop playing a role, a game, and be himself. A real person is a kind of "overwhelming majority" in interpersonal relationships. For example, a mother in one group was fearful of taking a definite stand on any issue involving her 14-year-old son. The son continued his unsuccessful attempts to get his mother to set a limit. Following several weeks of encouragement, she took a definite stand. The son now had something he could depend upon in place of great amounts of uncertainty. A real person is for sure.

4. The evaluation of meaning (sent and received) by each of the participants is established as a major concern by session six. This is the process by which we see individuals learn in the here-and-now of their experience. It is safe enough for them to expose their vulnerability to receive feedback from other persons in the TLC tradition, and to

relate in return their version of the perception that is discussed. In this process of dialogue, exchange of meanings becomes clarified so that individuals can more easily differentiate each other, as well as each self, from the rest of the group and the learning environment. Learning how to learn under these conditions is transferable to the larger culture because it is produced in a real-life laboratory. Personal meaning is a consequence of both affective and cognitive content and process. (See *double-bind*, Chapter 3.)

Session Six, Eight and Twelve: A Reiteration

The sessions conducted beyond session six become, in effect, a duplicate operation or continuation of what happens in session six. Providing the maturity of the group has reached a significant level of interaction by session six, the process is systematically continued until individual members of the family have achieved the level of proficiency they would hope to gain from their participation in family consultation.

A policy of furlough for the family at the end of session twelve should be established. It is not, necessarily, a final closure of the relationship. The relationship certainly should be interrupted for a period of time in order for the family to utilize what it has learned. The family should experiment, or try out those things that it has gained which are new. The learnings a family acquires are of no value until they can be utilized in the here-and-now of their existence. Such learning seems to have a separation point beyond which the individuals do not actually continue to gain. After time has elapsed, a family may reach a higher level of maturity, particularly in being able to gain access to, and utilize the help from, other resource persons.

1. Information gathering continues to be an incidental factor in the process of family consultation in all sessions beyond session five. There is a continuing concern for new information about the life events that have transpired since the beginning sessions. Most of this material will be kept current because of the enthusiasm of an individual for those things which are uppermost in his life space at the moment. However, those things which occur that are negative are sometimes buried because of the pain experienced in expressing them openly in a group. Besides, it is difficult to disappoint those people who have now come to expect certain forms of behavior even when they were associated with previous failure.

2. The identification of issues of concern to a family in the continuing sessions of family consultation are of major importance. One of those consists of the concern about success and failure. Failure is a very difficult procedure to manage in family consultation. It is a depressing note when a family member must report a failure in the group. The

group will usually redouble its efforts to offer support and constructive criticism to the individual family member. While these things are helpful, the basic pattern of failure must be interpreted by the counselors as an example of having taken too big a step (or permitted someone else to overextend). Evaluation of the counselor's leadership must always be a part of any reported failure on the part of an individual family member in family consultation. Sending and receiving messages and their meanings for participants continues to be as much a counselor responsibility as family member obligation (expectancy). Counselors spend time in group sessions checking on the meanings being exchanged by making certain the message *sent* is congruent with the message *received*. Counselor failure can be easily bypassed because the members of the group *expect* the counselor, as a leader and authority, to be more or less infallible. Our use of two or more counselors is based upon just such conditions of interaction distortions. The best arrangements seem to be to have a continuing evaluation of counselor leadership built into family consultation. How are you going to use what you have learned?

Success is a difficult issue for an entirely different set of reasons. Among this set of reasons is the emphasis upon the inability of most individuals to manage their own feelings when they have comprehended success in their life pattern. The feedback from other members in the family group consultation session may reflect concern about whether they will have equal success. One of the ways of managing this is for the counselors to take very little note of failure in order that a *neutral* position regarding these issues may be continued in the family sessions. This is a form of modeling behavior that may be important learning for individual members of family consultation if they are to learn successful ways of managing reactions to both failure and success.

3. The commitment of individual members within a family to family consultation is comparatively easy by the beginning of session six. Such evaluation must be made on a continuing basis because of the relative shift in the behavior-modification-relationship pattern within a family due to their progress in family consultation. It is not *unusual* to find that one person has achieved a difficult position because someone else has changed the way he reacts, acts, or relates to the other person. The commitment of the individual who is put at a disadvantage will usually change. This may be the first clue counselors will get that progress is being made by one or more other members in the family. One mother shifted her symbiosis from child A to child B. The result was quite dramatic. Child B ran away from home. Child A was no longer spending time in juvenile court. The mother became

the identified problem. Help for the mother became the new focus in family consultation.

4. A continuation of the description of events occurs as a regular format in family consultation. By the time the sixth or seventh session has passed, individual family members will begin interaction immediately upon assembly. The person who speaks first will have the floor and will be able to relate what is on his mind or what is concerning him at the moment. He desires some interaction, feedback, clarification and evaluation from other members.

5. From session six, seven, eight and so on, the consultative process is a continuing issue. The individual, who has learned how to *consult* with other persons in order to gain feedback in a form that is usable to him, has achieved a working relationship within the consultative process. This continues for each of the sessions of family consultation.

6. Alternative ways of behaving are discussed in each session in regard to each event and each report by each individual. Alternative ways of behaving represent the versatility and flexibility aspect of behavior to be learned in family consultation.

7. Changes are considered a usual part of the ongoing process of family consultation. It should be remembered that change is the introduction of ambiguity resulting from newly established relationships replacing the old and habitual or conditioned ways of responding to life events. It is important to note that individuals who experience changed behavior also experience a release of energy because of the excitement that usually results from a confirming experience.

Sessions Eight to Twelve:

By the time family group consultation has achieved session eight or twelve, it is possible to discuss openly with the family the desirability of entering into changed relationships. Change becomes partly a conscious choice in the problem solving behavior of the individuals within a family, and indeed, among families, as they develop peer relationships, one family to another, one individual to another. As this point, the counselors are only a kind of participant-observer in the family consultation process. Leadership should have long since passed to the significant members of the family.

Change is learning. Learning constitutes change. A useful example of this principle is the conventional wisdom in our culture that, once we have left our childhood home, we can never go back. Our changed perceptions remove the past because we have learned new concepts, have had new experiences. Family consultation achieves a similar quality of behavior modification.

Open Issues in Consultation

We have left the discussion of the issues related to family consultation open for the reader. There are several. Among the obvious is whether family consultation constitutes an appropriate activity in a school setting. Again, obviously, we think it does. To some counselors in educational settings only one-to-one counseling is possible. Our group counseling orientation allows for inclusion of many "others" in the counseling and consulting rooms. Let us presume that if you have read this far in this monograph, you must be interested in finding more resources and references to help your developing opinion become more viable. Following are a few annotated references that may be helpful.

BIBLIOGRAPHY

American Women. Report of the President's Commission on the Status of Women. Washington: Superintendent of Documents, U.S. Government Printing Office, 1963.

Arbuckle, D., "A Semantic Excursion." *Personnel and Guidance Journal,* Vol. 41, 1962, pp. 64–66.

Bell, N. W., and Vogel, E. F., eds., *A Modern Introduction to the Family.* New York: Free Press of Glencoe (Macmillan Co.), 1960.

Bernard, H. W., *Human Development in Western Culture,* 2nd ed. Boston: Allyn and Bacon, 1966.

Bower, E. M., "A Psychologist Views the Preparation and Potential of an Elementary School Counselor." A paper delivered at the Invitational Conference on Elementary School Guidance, U.S. Office of Education, Washington, D.C., 1965.

Bronfenbrenner, U., "Developmental Theory in Transition." In National Society for the Study of Education, 62nd Yearbook, Part I: *Child Psychology.* Chicago: University of Chicago Press, 1963, pp. 517–542.

Butler, J. L., Lecture to the NDEA Counseling and Guidance Institute, Portland Oregon, July 6, 1966.

————, Lecture, University of Oregon Medical School, Psychiatric Outpatient Clinic Sessions, Portland, Oregon, May 27, 1963.

Caldwell, B. M., "The Effects of Infant Care." In M. L. Hoffman and L. W. Hoffman, eds., *Review of Child Development Research,* Vol. I. New York: Russell Sage Foundation, 1964, pp. 9–87.

Coleman, J., "Social Change — Impact on the Adolescent." *National Association of Secondary School Principals Bulletin,* Vol. 49, 1965, pp. 11–14.

Combs, A. W., and Snygg, D., *Individual Behavior, A Perceptual Approach to Behavior.* New York: Harper and Row, 1959.

Fellin, P., "A Reappraisal of Changes in American Family Patterns." *Social Casework,* Vol. 45, 1964, pp. 263–267.

Finder, Morris, *A Structural View of English.* Boston: Ginn and Company, 1966.

Frank, L. K., *Personality and Culture: The Psychocultural Approach.* Danville, Illinois: The Interstate Printers and Publishers, 1948.

Frazier, E. F., *The Negro Family in the United States.* Chicago: University of Chicago Press, 1939.

Friedman, A. S., "The Family and Schizophrenia." In A. S. Friedman, et al., *Psychotherapy for the Whole Family.* New York: Springer Publishing Co., 1965.

Fullmer, D. W., and Bernard, H. W., *Counseling: Content and Process.* Chicago: Science Research Associates, 1966.

Gaddis, T. E., *Birdman of Alcatraz.* New York: Random House, 1955.

Haley, J., "The Family of the Schizophrenic: A Model System." *Journal of Nervous and Mental Disease,* Vol. 129, 1959, pp. 357–374.

Hall, E. T., *The Silent Language.* New York: Doubleday, 1959.

Harlow, H. F., and Harlow, M. K., "Social Deprivation in Monkeys." *Scientific American,* Vol. 207, 1962, pp. 136–146.

Irish, G., *Behavioral Changes of Participants in Family Group Consultation.* Corvallis, Oregon: Oregon State University, 1966. (Unpublished dissertation.)

Kelly, G., "Anthropology." In B. F. Hoselitz, ed., *A Reader's Guide to the Social Sciences.* New York: Free Press of Glencoe (Macmillan Co.), 1959.

Kluckhohn, C., "Common Humanity and Diverse Cultures." In D. Lerner, ed., *The Human Meaning of the Social Sciences.* Cleveland: World Publishing Co., 1959.

Lamberti, Armand, "A Type of Peer Relationship in a Girls' Training School." *Bulletin of the Menninger Clinic,* Vol. 27, 1963, pp. 200–204.

Lewin, K., and Grabbe, P., "Conduct, Knowledge, and Acceptance of New Values." *Journal of Social Issues,* Vol. 1, 1945, pp. 56–64.

Litwak, E., "Geographic Mobility and Extended Family Cohesion." *American Sociological Review.* Vol. 25, 1960, pp. 385–394.

Loban, W., "A Thirteen Year Longitudinal Study of Language Development in 210 Children from a Representative Sampling of Social-Economic-Caste Classes." Lecture, Portland, Oregon, Public School Principals, 1966.

Maslow, A. H., *Motivation and Personality.* New York: Harper and Row, 1954.

McCully, C. H., "Conceptions of Man and the Helping Professions." *Personnel and Guidance Journal,* Vol. 44, 1966, pp. 911–918.

Mead, M., and Heyman, K., *Family.* New York: Macmillan Co., 1965.

Mitchell, H. E., "The Continuing Search For a Conceptual Model of Family Pathology." In A. S. Friedman, et. al., *Psychotherapy for the Whole Family.* New York: Springer Publishing Co., 1965.

Murdock, G. P., "The Universality of the Nuclear Family." In N. W. Bell and E. F. Vogel, eds., *A Modern Introduction to the Family.* New York: Free Press of Glencoe (Macmillan Co.), 1960.

Pettigrew, T. F., *A Profile of the Negro American.* Princeton, New Jersey: D. Van Nostrand Co., 1964.

Prescott, D., Lecture, NDEA Counseling and Guidance Institute. Portland, Oregon, 1966.

Riessman, F., *The Culturally Deprived Child.* New York: Harper and Row, 1962.

Rogers, C. R., "The Place of the Person in the New World of the Behavioral Sciences." *Personnel and Guidance Journal,* Vol. 39, 1961, pp. 442–451.

Saslow, George, Lecture, NDEA Counseling and Guidance Institute. Portland, Oregon, May 16, 1966.

Schofield, W., "Education and Family Conflict." Lecture, Morningside Hospital, Portland, Oregon, May, 1966.

Spiro, M. E., "Is the Family Universal? — The Israeli Case." In N. W. Bell, and E. F. Vogel, eds., *A Modern Introduction to the Family.* New York: Free Press of Glencoe (Macmillan Co.), 1960.

Super, D. E., et al., *Career Development: Self-Concept Theory.* New York: College Entrance Examination Board, 1963.

The Negro Family: The Case for National Action. Washington: Superintendent of Documents, U.S. Government Printing Office, 1965.

Tyler, R. W., "Study Center for Behavioral Scientists." *Science,* Vol. 123, 1956, pp. 405–408.

U.S. Bureau of Census, Current Population Series, 1964, p. 20.

ANNOTATED BIBLIOGRAPHY

....

Ackerman, N. W., "The Unity of the Family." *Archives of Pediatrics*, Vol. 55, 1963.

Ackerman has published a number of very good source materials on the family. *The Psychodynamics of Family Life,* Basic Books, 1958, completes his twenty years of reporting. There are some additional recent writings that may be of interest to a student of family consultation.

Bateson, G. D., Jackson, D., Haley, J., and Weakland, J., "Toward a Theory of Schizophrenia." *Behavioral Science,* Vol. 1, 1956.

During the ten years following 1956, much literature accumulated about family counseling. Some basic ideas have come from the authors included above.

Bell, N. W., "Extended Family Relations of Disturbed and Well Families." *Family Process,* Vol. 1, 1962.

New journals appear to carry reports about methods and results from work with families. Much of the literature deals with sick families. Little is reported about well or healthy families. We do not know for sure if the two types are alike or different.

Eysenck, H. J., "The Effects of Psychotherapy." *International Journal of Psychiatry.* Vol. 1, 1965.

Eysenck elaborates eight major conclusions about psychotherapy derived from the literature. He has some strong arguments concerning whether psychotherapy really makes any difference to a patient. The implications for teaching and counseling are especially appropriate for the several issues one may raise about family consultation.

Friedman, A. S., et al., *Psychotherapy for the Whole Family.* New York: Springer Publishing Company, 1965.

A team of specialists in the applied behavioral sciences report on experiences they had with treatment of families of schizophrenic patients within the home of the patient. Treatment and teaching become closely related in the practice of psychotherapy in groups. Family groups are complex groups. Intervention and influence are among the important issues. Friedman, et al., have something to say on these and other issues.

Handel, G., *A Study of Family and Personality*. Unpublished doctoral dissertation, University of Chicago, 1962.

The personality of an individual may be the same as the personality of his family. This idea and the notions that seem to flow from it make possible a new set of interests.

Lewin, K., Lippitt, R., and White, R. K., "Patterns of Aggressive Behavior in Experimentally Created 'Social Climates.' " *Journal of Social Psychology*. Vol. 10, 1939.

The family is a socializing agent for society. How does the emotional climate in a family affect behavior in children? Can the school become an agent for change in family influence as a friend of the child? We hope you will read further in the many available reports. We even hope you will try family consultation. We did. It is a touching experience!

McGregor, R., et al., *Multiple Impact Therapy With Families*. New York: McGraw-Hill Book Company, 1964.

The report covers experiences of a Texas Medical Group using a team of specialists approach with families. The aim was to tap the self-rehabilitative powers within a family. The reader may gain insights about the nature of families as seen by McGregor, et al., and also find help with comprehending the issues connected with studying the families.

INDEX